C000118809

Planning Law

FOURTH EDITION

CLIVE BRAND

LLB, SOLICITOR

SERIES EDITOR
CM BRAND, SOLICITOR

Cavendish
Publishing
Limited

Fourth edition published in Great Britain 2001 by Cavendish Publishing Limited, The Glass House, Wharton Street, London WC1X 9PX, United Kingdom

Telephone: +44 (0)20 7278 8000   Facsimile: +44 (0)20 7278 8080

Email: info@cavendishpublishing.com

Website: www.cavendishpublishing.com

© Brand, C   2001

British Library Cataloguing in Publication Data

Brand, Clive M
Planning Law – 4th ed – (Practice notes series)
1 Planning – law and legislation – England 2 Land use – law and legislation – England   3 Planning – law and legislation – Wales
4 Land use – law and legislation – Wales
I Title
346.4'2'045

ISBN 1 85941 454 0

Printed and bound in Great Britain

Contents

1 Basic Information

1.1 Introduction

The function of this introductory chapter is to direct the reader to the essential materials that are needed in order to deal with a matter which arises under the town and country planning legislation. This may involve a range of different issues, for example, determining whether planning permission is needed, applying for planning permission, making an appeal following refusal of planning permission, opposing the development proposals of another party, or defending enforcement proceedings. On other occasions questions may arise as a result of the impact of town and country planning legislation on a conveyancing transaction. Giving the right advice and taking the appropriate action requires a knowledge both of town and country planning law and of practical considerations. First, a description must be given of the legislation which regulates the subject. This is followed by other sources including case law.

1.2 Sources

1.2.1 Statutes

The principal enactment is the Town and Country Planning Act 1990 ('the 1990 Act'), which is a consolidating Act. Further substantive law is to be found in two associated Acts: the Planning (Listed Buildings and Conservation Areas) Act 1990 and the Planning (Hazardous Substances) Act 1990. All three Acts came into force together on 24 August 1990. The 1990 legislation has, however, been amended in a number of significant respects (particularly in relation to enforcement of planning control) by the Planning and Compensation Act 1991. Local government structural changes effected by the Local Government (Wales) Act 1994 and the Environment Act 1995 (which enabled the establishment of National Park Authorities) have also necessitated many amendments to the 1990 Act. To ensure that reference is made to the current text, it will be necessary to have access to *The Encyclopedia of Planning Law and Practice* (see Chapter 10, 'Further Reading').

The most important sections of the Town and Country Planning Act 1990 are as follows:

Sections

1   specifies which authorities in England and Wales are local planning authorities and confers powers on county councils, district councils, metropolitan district councils, London borough councils and county borough councils;

4A   enables the establishment of National Park Authorities to act as local planning authorities within the National Parks;

12   requires preparation of a unitary development plan by each metropolitan district council and each London borough council;

27   meaning of 'development plan' in Greater London or a metropolitan county;

27A   meaning of 'development plan' in relation to Wales;

32   confers power on county councils to alter or replace an existing structure plan;

36   requires preparation of district-wide local plans by non-metropolitan district councils;

54   meaning of 'development plan' outside Greater London or a metropolitan county;

54A   planning decisions to be made in accordance with the development plan;

55   definition of 'development';

57   specifies that planning permission is required for the carrying-out of any development of land;

59   requires the Secretary of State (for the Environment) to make a 'development order' which grants planning permission for specified forms of development and (in all other cases) to make provision for applications for planning permission to be made to the local planning authority;

62   specifies that applications for planning permission shall be made in the prescribed manner;

191   application for certificate of lawfulness of existing use or development;

192   certificate of lawfulness of proposed use or development;

195   right of appeal to the Secretary of State against refusal of an application for a certificate under ss 191 and 192;

198   making of tree preservation orders;

215   power to require proper maintenance of land where amenity is adversely affected;

220   control of display of advertisements;

226   power to acquire land compulsorily for development purposes;

288   application to the High Court to quash specified planning orders and decisions;

289   appeal to the High Court against a decision of the Secretary of State in enforcement proceedings;

320   power of the Secretary of State to convene a public local inquiry;

336   definition section.

Readers of this book will also have cause to consult the Planning (Listed Buildings and Conservation Areas) Act 1990. The key provisions of that Act are as follows:

Sections

1   listing of buildings of special architectural or historic interest;

3   temporary listing by means of a building preservation notice;

8   authorisation of works to listed buildings;

10   making of applications for listed building consent;

20   right of appeal to the Secretary of State on refusal of listed building consent or grant subject to conditions;

38   power to issue a listed building enforcement notice;

47   compulsory acquisition of listed buildings;

69   designation of conservation areas;

72   requirement that special attention be paid to the desirability of preserving or enhancing the character or appearance of a conservation area in exercise of functions under the Planning Acts;

74   conservation area consent for demolition of buildings in conservation areas;

91   definition section.

1.2.2 Statutory instruments

Delegated legislation plays a key role in town and country planning as there are well over 100 different statutory instruments (quite apart from commencement orders) currently in force. Of these, only four have a direct effect on the substantive law of development control. These are:

(a) the Town and Country Planning (Applications) Regulations 1988 SI 1988/1812;

(b) the Town and Country Planning (General Permitted Development) Order 1995 SI 1995/418 (in this book referred to as 'the GPDO 1995');

(c) the Town and Country Planning (General Development Procedure) Order 1995 SI 1995/419 (in this book referred to as 'the GDPO 1995');

(d) the Town and Country Planning (Use Classes) Order 1987 SI 1987/764, as amended.

Another well-defined group of statutory instruments deals with the conduct of a planning or enforcement appeal. In this group are:

(a) the Town and Country Planning (Inquiries Procedure) (England) Rules 2000 SI 2000/1624;

(b) the Town and Country Planning (Determination by Inspectors) (Inquiries Procedure) (England) Rules 2000 SI 2000/1625;

(c) the Town and Country Planning (Hearings Procedure) (England) Rules 2000 SI 2000/1626;

(d) the Town and Country Planning (Appeals) (Written Representations Procedure) (England) Regulations 2000 SI 2000/1628;

(e) the Town and Country Planning (Enforcement) (Inquiries Procedure) Rules 1992 SI 1992/1903;

(f) the Town and Country Planning (Determination of Appeals by Appointed Persons) (Prescribed Classes) Regulations 1997 SI 1997/420.

Other principal regulations are those which regulate the control of advertisements:

(a) the Town and Country Planning (Control of Advertisements) Regulations 1992 SI 1992/666.

The payment of fees on making a planning application or an appeal against an enforcement notice are regulated by:

(b) the Town and Country Planning (Fees for Applications and Deemed Applications) Regulations 1989 (SI 1989/193, as amended by SI 1990/2473, SI 1991/2735, SI 1992/1817, SI 1992/3052, SI 1993/3170 and SI 1997/37).

1.2.3 Departmental circulars and policy guidance

The Department of the Environment, Transport and the Regions frequently issues circulars and planning policy guidance notes. These documents explain the powers and duties of local planning authorities, explain the effect of new legislation and give guidance on national planning policy. Circulars tend to focus on legislative and procedural matters. Leading examples of these are:

(a) 13/87 Change of Use of Buildings and Other Land: Town and Country Planning (Use Classes) Order 1987;

(b) 14/91 Planning and Compensation Act 1991;

(c) 15/92 Publicity for Planning Applications;

(d) 8/93 Award of Costs Incurred in Planning and Other (Including Compulsory Purchase Order) Proceedings;

(e) 9/95 General Development Order Consolidation 1995;

(f) 10/95 Planning Controls over Demolition;

(g) 11/95 The Use of Conditions in Planning Permissions;

(h) 1/97 Planning Obligations;

(i) 10/97 Enforcing Planning Control: Legislative Provisions and Procedural Requirements;

(j) 2/99 Environmental Impact Assessment;

(k) 05/2000 Planning Appeals: Procedures (Including Inquiries into Called-in Planning Applications).

Planning policy guidance notes are:

(a) PPG 1 General Policy and Principles;

(b) PPG 2 Green Belts;

(c) PPG 3 Housing;

(d) PPG 4 Industrial and Commercial Development and Small Firms;

(e) PPG 5 Simplified Planning Zones;

(f) PPG 6 Town Centres and Retail Developments;

(g) PPG 7 The Countryside: Environmental Quality and Economic and Social Development;

(h) PPG 8 Telecommunications;

(i) PPG 9 Nature Conservation;

(j) PPG 10 Planning and Waste Management;

(k) PPG 11 [deleted];

(l) PPG 12 Development Plans;

(m)PPG 13 Transport;

(n) PPG 14 Development on Unstable Land;

(o) PPG 15 Planning and the Historic Environment;

(p) PPG 16 Archaeology and Planning;

(q) PPG 17 Sport and Recreation;

(r) PPG 18 Enforcing Planning Control;

(s) PPG 19 Outdoor Advertisement Control;

(t) PPG 20 Coastal Planning;

(u) PPG 21 Tourism;

(v) PPG 22 Renewable Energy;

(w)PPG 23 Planning and Pollution Control;

(x) PPG 24 Planning and Noise.

Practitioners should also note relevant regional or strategic guidance for their area contained in a series of regional planning guidance documents. These are:

(a) RPG 1 Strategic Guidance for Tyne and Wear;

(b) RPG 2 Strategic Guidance for West Yorkshire;

(c) RPG 3 Strategic Guidance for London Planning Authorities;

(d) RPG 4 Strategic Guidance for Greater Manchester;

(e) RPG 5 Strategic Guidance for South Yorkshire;

(f) RPG 6 Regional Planning Guidance for East Anglia;

(g) RPG 7 Regional Planning Guidance for the Northern Region;

(h) RPG 8 Regional Planning Guidance for the East Midlands Region;

(i) RPG 9 Regional Planning Guidance for the South East;

(j) RPG 9A The Thames Gateway Planning Framework;

(k) RPG 10 Regional Planning Guidance for the South West;

(l) RPG 11 Regional Planning Guidance for the West Midlands Region;

(m)RPG 12 Regional Planning Guidance for Yorkshire and Humberside;

(n) RPG 13 Regional Planning Guidance for the North West.

The above circulars and policy guidance are essential reading in understanding planning practice and procedures and therefore repay close examination both for the purposes of giving advice on planning matters and also in preparing for planning appeals.

1.2.4 Cases

The current town and country planning system is derived from the Town and Country Planning Act 1947 which came into force on 1 July 1948. As more than 50 years have elapsed since that date, a very substantial body of case law has developed. Access to this case law is achieved by using the conventional research methods.

Decisions of the superior courts are, however, one source of the planning case law. A further other source is planning appeal decisions issued by the Secretary of State for the Environment, Transport and the Regions. These do not have binding effect but will frequently contain opinion on the interpretation of a point of law and are useful, persuasive authority in argument. These can be sourced from Planning Appeal Decisions and the several journals mentioned in Chapter 10.

1.3   Administrative authorities

The authorities entrusted with the administration of the town and country planning system are principally the local planning authorities and the Secretary of State for the Environment, Transport and the Regions. The former are the local authorities, district councils, county councils, London borough councils and, in Wales, county borough councils. It is these authorities which carry out the bulk of planning functions, especially the making of decisions on applications for planning permission. In this respect, the Secretary of State is an appellate authority, though the 1990 Act confers many other powers on the Secretary of State which are exercised independently of any action taken by a local planning authority. So far as planning applications are concerned, the framework, including the superior courts, is as follows:

(a) House of Lords;

(b) Court of Appéal;

(c) High Court (under s 288 of the 1990 Act (restricted right of appeal – does not include merits of decision);

(d) Secretary of State for the Environment;

(e) s 78 of the 1990 Act (unrestricted right of appeal – includes merits of decision);

(f) local planning authority (under s 70 of the 1990 Act (empowers local planning authority to determine a planning application)).

1.3.1 Powers of local planning authorities

To determine the powers of the local authority in relation to a particular parcel of land it is necessary first to determine the geographical location of the land. If it is contained within the area of a London borough council or in the area of a metropolitan district council (one contained within the metropolitan areas of Greater Manchester, Merseyside, West Midlands, Tyne and Wear, West Yorkshire and South Yorkshire) then all the powers conferred by the planning legislation on local planning authorities (LPAs) will be exercisable by these authorities. This is due to the single-tier nature of local government in these areas. Further areas of single-tier local government exist where powers have been exercised by the Secretary of State under the Local Government Act 1992, following recommendations in that behalf by the Local Government Commission. The effect is that many district councils in the 'shire counties' are unitary authorities. In some counties, all the district councils have unitary status; in other counties some of the districts are unitary authorities while the remainder are subject to the two-tier system established under the Local Government Act 1972. In the shire counties in which the two-tier arrangements are unaffected, both county councils and district councils have planning functions. These authorities are referred to in s 1(1) of the 1990 Act as the county planning authority (CPA) and the district planning authority (DPA), respectively.

The powers which LPAs exercise are detailed in s 1 of and Sched 1 to the 1990 Act: those which are particularly relevant to this book are summarised in the table below. In Wales, the relevant authorities are the county councils and the county borough councils; these authorities provide a single tier of local government in accordance with the Local Government (Wales) Act 1994.

The distribution of functions between CPAs and DPAs depends to a large extent on whether a 'county matter' is involved. County matters comprise a small group of development activities listed in para 1 of Sched 1 to the 1990 Act and the Town and County Planning (Prescription of County Matters) Regulations 1980 SI 1980/2010. These are (broadly) mineral-related developments and deposit on land of refuse or waste materials. It must be noted, however, that some functions exercised by DPAs are exercisable concurrently with CPAs. Examples of such concurrent powers are the designation of conservation areas under s 69 of the Planning (Listed Buildings and Conservation Areas) Act 1990, and compulsory acquisition of land for development under s 226 of the 1990 Act.

Principal functions of LPAs

Function	London borough councils and metropolitan district councils, Welsh county councils and county borough councils	Non-metropolitan district councils	Shire county councils
Development plan	Unitary development plan	Local plan	Structure plan
Planning applications	All applications	Most applications (except 'county matters')	Some applications (only 'county matters')
Enforcement of planning control	All breaches of planning control	Almost all breaches of planning control (except a limited class of 'county matters')	Some breaches of planning control (only 'county matters')
Advertisement applications	All applications	All applications	None
Applications for certificates of lawfulness of proposed use or development	All determinations	Most determinations (except 'county matters')	Some determinations (only 'county matters')
Applications for certificates of lawfulness of existing use or development	All applications	Most applications (except 'county matters')	Some applications (only 'county matters')
Applications for listed building consent	All applications	All applications	None
Maintenance of planning register	All applications and decisions	All applications and decisions	None

1.3.2 Powers of the Secretary of State

The Secretary of State is the appellate authority in planning control, although he also exercises a number of confirmatory and 'first instance' powers. His appeal functions (in relation to the 1990 Act) are primarily in respect of:

(a) s 78 appeals against refusal by the LPA to grant planning permission, or against a grant subject to conditions;

(b) s 174 appeals against issue by the LPA of an enforcement notice;

(c) s 195 appeals against refusal by the LPA to issue a certificate of lawfulness of proposed use or development, or certificate of lawfulness of existing use or development; and

(d) s 220 appeals against refusal by the LPA to grant consent for the display of an advertisement, or against a grant subject to conditions.

Powers to confirm action taken by LPAs include:

(a) s 98 power to confirm an order by the LPA effecting a revocation or modification of a grant of planning permission;

(b) s 103 power to confirm an order by the LPA requiring a use of land to be discontinued or that any buildings or works should be altered or removed; and

(c) s 226 power to confirm a compulsory purchase order made by the LPA for development purposes.

Powers of 'first instance' include:

(a) s 59 issue of development orders. It may be noted that the Secretary of State exercises many other delegated legislative powers, mostly exercised by statutory instrument but with occasional use of ministerial directions; and

(b) s 77 power to call in a planning application from the LPA for his own decision.

Further powers of 'first instance' are contained in s 1 of the Planning (Listed Buildings and Conservation Areas) Act 1990 (which concerns compilation of lists of buildings of special architectural or historic interest), and s 1 of the Ancient Monuments and Archaeological Areas Act 1979 (which concerns compilation of lists of monuments of national importance).

1.3.3 Other institutions with development control powers

In most areas of England and Wales, development control is effected through the LPAs described above.

Note should also be made in this context of the functions of the Urban Regeneration Agency (better known as 'English Partnerships') which was established by Pt III of the Leasehold Reform, Housing and Urban Development Act 1993. Like the urban development corporations (which were established under the Local Government, Planning and Land Act 1980 to achieve regeneration of designated urban development areas), the Agency also has regeneration functions, though the relevant powers are exercisable in respect of any land in England which is vacant or unused, or situated in an urban area and is under-used or ineffectively used, or contaminated, derelict, neglected or unsightly. The planning functions of the Agency in relation to any given area of land depend on the content of a designation order: not all planning functions will be exercised by the Agency, but the Agency will act as the local planning authority to the extent of such powers as are specified in the designation order.

A number of other authorities have planning functions. Those which are most likely to be of significance are National Park authorities established under the Environment Act 1995. To date, 10 such authorities have been established, initially in respect of the National Parks in Wales under the National Park Authorities (Wales) Order 1995 SI 1995/2803 and, subsequently, in respect of the National Parks in England under the National Park Authorities (England) Order 1996 SI 1996/1243.

In these areas, the planning powers of the relevant local authorities have been transferred pursuant to the relevant orders. The National Parks are the areas of Dartmoor, Exmoor, Snowdonia, Brecon Beacons, Pembrokeshire Coast, Northumberland, Yorkshire Dales, North Yorkshire Moors, Peak District and the Lake District.

1.4 Principal terms and scheme of development control

The basic premise of the planning system is that planning permission is required in order to carry out any development of land (s 57 of the 1990 Act). The key terms are discussed below.

1.4.1 'Development'

This is defined by s 55 as 'the carrying out of building, engineering, mining or other operations in, on, over or under land, or the making of any material change in the use of any buildings or other land'. This definition is clearly in two parts, a distinction being made between what is commonly termed 'operational development' (building, etc) and development comprising a material change of use. A great deal of literature has been generated by this definition and a good knowledge of its scope is essential, since in many cases it will not be necessary to make an application for planning permission.

Thus, no 'development' takes place in the following cases specified in s 55(2):

(a) works for maintenance, improvement or other alteration of a building which are only interior works or which do not materially affect the external appearance of the building;

(b) the use of any buildings or other land within the curtilage of a dwelling house for any purpose incidental to the enjoyment of the dwelling house as such;

(c) the use of any land for the purposes of agriculture or forestry (including afforestation) and the use for any of those purposes of any building occupied together with land so used;

(d) the change of use of buildings or land to another use of the same class specified in the Town and Country Planning (Use Classes) Order 1987 SI 1987/764. This crucial item of delegated legislation contains 11 different classes of use;

(e) demolition of buildings specified in the Town and Country Planning (Demolition Description of Buildings) Direction 1995 (for example, buildings other than a dwelling house or a building adjoining a dwelling house).

The following matters are deemed by s 55(3) to involve development requiring planning permission:

(a) the use as two or more separate dwelling houses of any building previously used as a single dwelling house (that is, use of a property converted to flats or maisonettes, including subdivision of existing flats or maisonettes);

(b) deposit refuse or waste materials on land.

In many instances, the proposal falls within the definition of 'development', but there is no need to make an application for planning permission because this is deemed to be granted by the Town and Country Planning (General Permitted Development) Order 1995 SI 1995/418. Consultation of Sched 2 to this Order (often referred to as the 'GPDO') shows that 84 classes of development are identified arranged in 33 Parts.

Some of these are of everyday importance to the practitioner, for example:

(a) Pt 1 Class A authorises construction of extensions to dwelling houses and other improvements, for example, construction of a garage, subject to a series of conditions and provisos, for example, imposing a maximum size on the development of 15% of the existing volume or 70 cubic metres, whichever is the greater, subject to an overall maximum of 115 cubic metres. Terraced houses (and, also, all houses in certain sensitive locations, for example, a conservation area) are subject to smaller tolerances (10% of the existing volume or 50 cubic metres, subject to the same overall maximum of 115 cubic metres).

In view of the many qualifications, particular care must be taken to be accurate in advising that Pt 1 Class A applies;

(b) Pt 2 Class A authorises construction of gates, fences and walls or other means of enclosure provided that they do not exceed one metre in height where abutting on a highway or two metres in height in any other case;

(c) other classes which are frequently consulted are Pts 3, 4, 6 and 8.

These deal with changes of use of buildings (Pt 3), temporary buildings and uses (Pt 4), agricultural buildings and operations (Pt 6) and industrial and warehouse development (Pt 8). The last of these examples includes extensions to industrial buildings. Such extensions are authorised provided the cubic content of the building is not increased by more than 25% and the aggregate floor space is not increased by more than 1,000 square metres. As with domestic developments, a number of conditions need to be complied with and, hence, careful consultation of Pt 8 is required when advising a client with an industrial undertaking. In addition, smaller tolerances apply (10% and 500 square metres) if the industrial building or warehouse is situated in the area of a National Park, an area of outstanding natural beauty, or a conservation area.

For further discussion of the definition of development see Brand and Williams, *Planning Law for Conveyancers,* 4th edn, pp 8–14, 111–24 and 147–51; these pages contain illustrations of the scope of the definition as well as a detailed examination of the GPDO 1995.

1.4.2 'Permitted development'

This is not formally defined but is the term used to describe any permission to develop land granted by the GPDO 1995 or a special development order.

1.4.3 'Planning permission'

This is not defined in any useful manner by the legislation. It was held, however, in *R v West Oxfordshire DC ex p Pearce (CH) Homes* (1986) JPL 523 that 'planning permission' is the document issued to a successful applicant by the LPA, as distinct from the resolution of the authority to grant planning permission.

1.4.4 'Enterprise zone'

An enterprise zone is an area designated by a district council or development corporation at the invitation of the Secretary of State for the Environment. The object is to stimulate industrial and commercial activity in the area. This is achieved by simplifying planning controls and conferring substantial financial advantages. The relevant legislation is s 179 of and Sched 32 to the Local Government, Planning and Land Act 1980, as amended by s 54 of the Housing and Planning Act 1986. Planning controls in an enterprise zone are relaxed to the extent specified in the enterprise zone scheme prepared by the zone authority (the district council or development corporation, whichever was invited to prepare the scheme), though by virtue of s 88 of the 1990 Act, such planning permission can be qualified by a direction of the zone authority issued with the prior approval of the Secretary of State. Enterprise zone designation lasts for 10 years.

1.4.5 'Simplified planning zone'

Under s 83 of the 1990 Act, LPAs are required to consider whether it would be desirable to simplify planning controls in any part(s) of their area. If so, a 'simplified planning zone scheme' will be prepared pursuant to Sched 7 to the 1990 Act in which development controls will be relaxed as specified by the scheme.

1.4.6 'Development plan'

This is formally defined by s 54 of the 1990 Act to comprise in relation to any district the structure plan, and any local plan applicable to the district and any alterations to these plans. The structure plan is a strategic document prepared by the county planning authority which formulates the authority's policy and general proposals in respect of the development and other use of land. Local plans are much more specific being in the form of a map and written statement. These documents are available for public inspection and copies may be obtained from the LPA for a reasonable charge. To advise clients fully and effectively, it is essential to maintain office copies of these documents.

In the area of each London borough council and metropolitan district council, the development plan described above is superseded by a 'unitary development plan' prepared pursuant to s 12 of the 1990 Act. As the name implies this is a single plan incorporating features of structure and local plans.

1.4.7 'Breach of planning control'

If an act of development is carried out without a grant of planning permission where such a grant is required, or if development takes place in breach of a condition or limitation attached to a grant of planning permission then, according to s 171A of the 1990 Act, the developer is in breach of planning control. Where a breach occurs, the LPA may take enforcement action by issue of an enforcement notice or a breach of condition notice.

1.4.8 'Enforcement notice'

Where there has been a breach of planning control, the LPA is empowered by s 172 of the 1990 Act to require the breach to be remedied by issue of a notice to that effect. Such a notice is expressly termed an enforcement notice (s 172(1)). Such a notice will state the matters which the LPA consider to constitute the breach of planning control and the steps necessary to remedy it.

1.4.9 'Breach of condition notice'

Where the breach of planning control consists of failure to comply with a condition attached to a grant of planning permission, s 187A of the 1990 Act enables the LPA to serve a breach of condition notice as an alternative to the issue of an enforcement notice. This is a summary method of control since there is no right of appeal against a breach of condition notice, unlike an enforcement notice which can be the subject of an appeal to the Secretary of State for the Environment.

1.4.10 'Planning contravention notice'

In order to prepare to take enforcement action, the LPA will wish to obtain information in relation to operations being carried out on the land, any use of the land or matters relating to conditions. This research is aided by the issue of this notice under s 171C of the 1990 Act, since relevant information can be required of the owner or occupier of the land or any person carrying out operations on it or using it for any purpose. Failure to comply with the requirements of a planning contravention notice is an offence.

1.4.11 'Established use certificate'

A limitation period of four years once applied to all breaches of planning control. Currently, the four-year limitation period only applies to 'operational' development and to the making of a material change of use of a building to use as a single dwelling house (s 171B). Until the coming into force of the Planning and Compensation Act 1991, it followed that all other material changes of use which were in breach of planning control were vulnerable to enforcement action whenever they first occurred. Some of these developments, however, gained the benefit of the four-year limitation rule before it was altered in 1968. Such a development may have been the subject of an established use certificate issued by the LPA under s 191 of the 1990 Act before that provision was repealed and replaced by the Act of 1991. Although established use certificates are now superseded by certificates of lawful use or development, they will remain of significance in the context of enforcement proceedings.

1.4.12 'Certificate of lawful use or development'

An unauthorised use of, or operational development on land becomes lawful when no enforcement action can be taken in respect of it. As noted above, operational development becomes immune from enforcement action once the four-year limitation period has expired. This also applies to a material change of use comprising a change of use of a building to use as a single dwelling house. All other material changes of use are subject to a 10-year limitation rule specified in s 171B of the 1990 Act, a rule which also applies to a failure to comply with a condition or limitation subject to which planning permission has previously been granted. In order to have a development certified as lawful by passage of time, s 191 of the 1990 Act (as substituted by the 1991 Act) provides for application to the LPA for a certificate of lawful use or development.

1.4.13 'Listed building'

This term is a convenient statutory abbreviation for the term 'building of special architectural or historic interest'. Both terms appear in s 1 of the Planning (Listed Buildings and Conservation Areas) Act 1990 which places the Secretary of State under a duty to compile lists of such buildings with a view to their protection from demolition or alteration or extension.

1.4.14 'Conservation area'

Section 69 of the Planning (Listed Buildings and Conservation Areas) Act 1990 places LPAs under a duty to determine which parts of their area are 'of special architectural or historic interest the character or appearance of which it is desirable to preserve or enhance'. Any area which the LPA considers is in this category is then designated as a conservation area by a resolution of the LPA. This has a number of consequences, for example, more restrictive development control and the need for 'conservation area consent' for demolition of unlisted buildings in the area.

1.4.15 'National Park'

Under s 6 of the National Parks and Access to the Countryside Act 1949, the Countryside Agency (formerly the Countryside Commission) is required to designate extensive tracts of country in England for the purpose of:

(a) conserving and enhancing the natural beauty, wildlife and cultural heritage of the designated areas; and

(b) promoting opportunities for the understanding and enjoyment by the public of the special quality of those areas.

Development control in these areas is accordingly very restrictive. Equivalent powers are exercised in respect of Wales by the Countryside Council for Wales.

1.4.16 'Area of outstanding natural beauty'

Such an area is designated by the Countryside Agency (or, in Wales, by the Countryside Council for Wales) under s 87 of the National Parks and Access to the Countryside Act 1949. The area will be less extensive than that of a National Park but the development control consequences are similar.

2 Planning Application Procedures

2.1 Introduction

In this chapter, guidance is given on the steps which need to be taken and how to proceed in the most frequently occurring matters involving an application under the town and country planning legislation. These are:

(a) making an application for planning permission;

(b) seeking a determination whether planning permission is required;

(c) applying for listed building or conservation area consent.

Advice is also given on a fourth matter: opposing the development proposals of another party. Even before a client with a 'planning problem' enters your office, you need to be prepared for coping with planning matters, not merely by having the appropriate library of commercial publications (see Chapter 10, 'Further Reading') but by gathering together useful documentation which has been issued by the local planning authority (LPA), or by the Secretary of State for the Environment, Transport and the Regions. You should therefore have office copies of the following documents:

(a) the structure plan;

(b) any local plans, whether comprising a district plan, subject plan, or action area plan;

(c) the unitary development plan if your practice is in a London borough, a metropolitan district, within a unitary authority area or in Wales. If the development plan is in the process of being revised, obtain copies of the current draft documents relating to the proposed plan if it has not yet been adopted by the LPA. You should also obtain any supplementary planning guidance issued by the LPA, for example, (1) in respect of design standards in respect of house extensions, new housing development, conversion to flats and (2) car parking standards;

(d) a supply of forms of application for planning permission;

(e) a supply of forms of application for listed building consent or conservation area consent.

The structure plan, the local plans and the unitary development plan (or documents associated with an emerging plan, for example, proposed modifications) may be the subject of a charge by the LPA.

2.2 Taking instructions

Much of the first meeting with the client will be devoted to obtaining as much information as possible about the proposed development, though the details which are recorded will be supplemented by further information which becomes available to you as you proceed to carry out instructions. It is advisable to compile a fact sheet of information to which you can refer. Rather than have different fact sheets for use with different types of application a composite document can be used. The following is a recommended draft.

Applications under the Town and Country Planning Act 1990: client fact sheet

Personal details

1   Client's full name

2   Address

3   Telephone number

(a) business

(b) home

4   Fax

5   Email

Property details

1   Property involved (address or site description) including area in hectares and acres and description of existing development and use of the property (if any)

2   Is the client sole owner of this property? Yes/No

3   If 'No', details of all other parties (for example, full name of co-owning spouse or business partner)

4   Address(es) of other co-owners

5 Is the client the tenant of the property? Yes/No

6 If 'Yes', name and address of landlord and of any agent (if known)

7 Is the property the subject of a tenancy granted by the client or former owner? Yes/No

8 If 'Yes', name(s) and address(es) of tenant(s)

9 Which tenant(s) have a lease with at least seven years unexpired?

10 When did the client acquire his/her interest in the property?

11 If the property is currently agricultural land is there an agricultural tenant? Yes/No

12 If 'Yes', name and address of tenant and of any agent (if known)

13 Is any building on the land listed as being of special architectural or historic interest?

14 Is any building on the land contained within a conservation area?

15 Is the property contained within a National Park or area of outstanding natural beauty?

16 Are there any trees on the land? Yes/No

17 If 'Yes', give details of species and number and location on a site plan

Professional advisors

1 Name of client's architect

2 Address

3 Telephone and fax numbers and email address

4 Reference

5 Name of client's surveyor

6 Address

7 Telephone and fax numbers and email address

8 Reference

Planning details

1 What provisions of the current development plan are relevant to the property?

2 Which other planning policy documents are relevant to the property or the proposed development?

3 What is the existing use of the property?

4 When did this use begin?

5   Give full details of the proposal (for example, whether building involved or material change of use, number of buildings, number of storeys, floorspace, etc)

6   Has planning permission for the current or other proposals ever been applied for before? Yes/No

7   If 'Yes', give details of proposals and decisions of the LPA

8   Has any other form of consent been applied for before, for example, listed building consent or conservation area consent? Yes/No

9   If 'Yes', give details of proposals and decisions of the LPA

10 Has the property ever been the subject of a planning or other appeal (for example, against an enforcement notice) to the Secretary of State? Yes/No

11 If 'Yes', give details

12 Are any decision letters available? (If in existence, but not available obtain from LPA)

13 How many people will be employed at the property . if the proposed development is carried out?

(a) full time

(b) part time

14 Will any person be resident at the property? Yes/No

15 If 'Yes', state how many

16 Calculate car parking requirements of:

(a) residents

(b) full time employees

(c) part time employees

(d) visitors, assuming busiest time of use of the property

17 Does the client own any adjacent or nearby property? Yes/No

18 If 'Yes', give details of current uses and existing consents

19 Is there a recent result of search in the register of local land charges and replies to Enquiries of the Local Authority? Yes/No

20 If 'No', requisition the relevant search (LLC 1) and submit Enquiries (Con 29)

Local Planning Authority (for use during follow-up)

1   Name of LPA

2   Telephone, fax numbers and email address of LPA

3   Name of planning officer dealing with application

4   Planning officer's telephone extension

5   Name of Planning Committee clerk

6   Committee clerk's telephone extension

The object of the first meeting is not only to obtain basic details for file purposes but, more especially, to determine what consents will be needed if the client's proposal is to be implemented. It will also be necessary to determine whether the application should be an application for outline planning permission or a detailed application and the relevant policy issues which are involved. Sometimes, the proposal will involve more than a grant of planning permission. Conversely, in some cases the client may not need a grant of planning permission but may nevertheless require other consents regulated by the town and country planning or associated legislation, for example, listed building consent or conservation area consent.

2.3   Determining whether planning permission is required

Whether planning permission is required is always the basic question to be answered before any other factors are considered. The starting point is to remind oneself of the broad scope of the definition of 'development' contained in s 55 of the Town and Country Planning Act 1990 (the '1990 Act'), that is, that development comprises 'building, engineering, mining or other operations in, on, over or under land or the making of any material change in the use of any building or other land'. Placed against this definition most proposals will constitute 'development', so one must then go on to examine whether it is necessary to make an application for planning permission to the LPA. This requires careful study of s 55 as a whole since some matters noted in Chapter 1 are expressly excluded, for example, interior works. It must also be considered whether the proposed development falls within the scope of the Town and Country Planning (General Permitted Development) Order 1995 or the Town and Country Planning (Use Classes) Order 1987, as these Orders will in many instances obviate the need to apply for planning permission for the forms of development specified in them. For more detailed information, reference can be made to these Orders together with any amendments which are relevant; these are reproduced in *The Encyclopedia of Planning Law and Practice* (see Chapter 10).

Even if the proposed development appears to be authorised by either of the above orders, planning permission may nevertheless still be necessary. This is because of the possible existence of any of the following:

(a) an Art 4 direction – the result of the local land charges search and replies to Enquiries of the Local Authority will reveal whether such a direction exists or is proposed. Under Art 4 of the GPDO 1995, the LPA or the Secretary of State can direct that normal permitted development tolerances be modified, thereby necessitating an application for planning permission. This is often done in sensitive locations such as conservation areas;

(b) a condition attached to a previous grant of planning permission which may attempt to take away permitted development rights under the GPDO 1995 – such a condition appears to be competent provided it is clear and unequivocal (*Dunoon Developments Ltd v Secretary of State for the Environment* (1992) JPL 936); or

(c) a condition attached to a previous grant of planning permission which may attempt to take away rights under the Use Classes Order – this has been held to be competent (*City of London Corp v Secretary of State for the Environment* (1971) 23 P & CR 169).

2.4 Determining whether other consents are required

In most cases, a grant of planning permission is sufficient to authorise the proposed development. It is, however, essential to be alert to the possibility that one or more further consents may be needed; in particular, because the proposed development involves work to a listed building or the proposal involves work to a building contained in a conservation area.

A listed building is one which has been entered by the Secretary of State in a list of buildings of special architectural or historic interest compiled under s 1 of the Planning (Listed Buildings and Conservation Areas) Act 1990. Once listed, it is an offence to carry out works to the building (including interior works) unless a grant of 'listed building consent' is obtained from the LPA under s 8 of that Act. Such an offence is punishable on summary conviction by a fine of up to £20,000 or by up to six months' imprisonment (or both). On conviction on indictment, the offence is punishable by an unlimited fine or by up to two years' imprisonment (or both). As this offence is one of strict liability (*R v Wells Street Metropolitan Stipendiary Magistrate ex p Westminster CC* [1986] 3 All ER 4), it is essential to determine whether this consent is necessary by consulting the result of the local land charges search.

Of a similar nature is the protection afforded to buildings contained within a conservation area. Such an area is designated by the LPA under s 69 of the Planning (Listed Buildings and Conservation Areas) Act 1990 as one of special architectural or historic interest, the character or appearance of which it is desirable to preserve or enhance. While some buildings within such an area will be listed under s 1 of that Act, most will not have a listed building status. In these instances 'conservation area consent' is required from the LPA under s 74 of the Planning (Listed Buildings and Conservation Areas) Act 1990 in order to demolish (but not to alter or extend). The penalties for failure to comply with this control are identical to those relating to breach of listed building control. To discover the existence of a conservation area designation affecting the property, regard must once again be had to the result of the local land charges search.

Other matters giving rise to the need for a further consent are summarised below. The details of the legislation are fully explained in *Planning Law for Conveyancers* (see Chapter 10) and a note on criminal penalties appears in Chapter 8 of this book:

(a) Development involving works to an ancient monument scheduled by the Secretary of State under s 1 of the Ancient Monuments and Archaeological Areas Act 1979. Consent known as 'scheduled monument consent' is required from the Secretary of State.

(b) Consent under a tree preservation order: LPAs are empowered to make tree preservation orders under s 198 of the 1990 Act. Any such order will prohibit the cutting down, topping, lopping, uprooting, wilful damage or wilful destruction of any tree to which it applies unless the consent of the LPA has been obtained. In a conservation area, all the trees within the area are subjected to an interim form of control unless specifically included in a tree preservation order: under s 211 the developer must give six weeks' notice to the LPA, thereby giving the LPA a final opportunity to make an order if they so desire.

(c) Development which involves bringing onto the land any 'hazardous substance' in excess of the 'controlled quantity' requires the consent of the hazardous substances authority under s 4 of the Planning (Hazardous Substances) Act 1990. A grant of 'hazardous substances consent' must be obtained from the district council or London borough. The scope of 'hazardous substance' and 'controlled quantity' is, in each case, detailed in the Planning (Hazardous Substances) Regulations 1992 SI 1992/656.

(d) Caravan sites are subject to a site licensing control under the Caravan Sites and Control of Development Act 1960. Under s 1 of this Act, a site licence is required to use any land for the purpose of stationing a caravan for human habitation. There are, however, many exceptions to this requirement, in respect of which see s 2 of and Sched 1 to the 1960 Act.

2.5 Planning applications

2.5.1 Notification to owners and agricultural tenants

In cases where the applicant for planning permission is not the sole owner of the land, notification of the making of the application must be served on all other owners. An 'owner' for these purposes includes a tenant who has a lease with at least seven years unexpired (s 65(8)). In addition, notice must be given to any agricultural tenant, irrespective of the tenant's unexpired term. The relevant persons entitled to notification are identified by reference to a date 21 days before the making of the application. Notification will normally be by means of service of a prescribed form of notice on each person entitled to receive notice; however, where reasonable steps have been taken to identify the names and addresses of such persons, but without success, resort must be made to newspaper notification. These requirements are mandatory since s 65(5) provides that the LPA 'shall not entertain' the application unless the requirements have been satisfied. The form of notice is prescribed by Art 6 and Sched 2, Pt 1 to the Town and Country Planning (General Development Procedure) Order 1995 SI 1995/419 (GDPO 1995). A certificate relating to ownership and, if necessary, compliance with these requirements is prescribed by Art 7 and Sched 2, Pt 2 to the GDPO 1995 (see Chapter 7).

Town and Country Planning (General Development Procedure) Order 1995: Notice under Art 6 of Application for Planning Permission

Proposed development at (a) *29 Monk Street, Worktown, Planshire*

I give notice that (b) *Richard Thomas*

is applying to the (c) *Worktown District Council*

for planning permission to (d) change the use of above premises to use as a building contractor's yard

Any owner of the land or tenant who wishes to make representations about this application should write to the Council at (e) *Town Hall, Victoria Road, Worktown*

by (f)

signed

On behalf of

Date

Statement of owners' rights

The grant of planning permission does not affect owners' rights to retain or dispose of their property, unless there is some provision to the contrary in an agreement or in a lease.

Statement of agricultural tenants' rights

The grant of planning permission for non-agricultural development may affect agricultural tenants' security of tenure. Insert:

(a) address or location of the proposed development;

(b) applicant's name;

(c) name of council;

(d) description of the proposed development;

(e) address of the council;

(f) date giving a period of 21 days beginning with the date of service, or 14 days beginning with the date of publication, of the notice (as the case may be).

2.5.2 Preparation and submission of the application

To make an application for planning permission it is necessary to submit to the LPA the following, as prescribed by s 62 of the 1990 Act and Art 3 of the Town and Country Planning (Applications) Regulations 1988:

(a) application form – this is not a prescribed form but the application will be made on such form as is provided by the LPA;

(b) site plan – this is required to identify the land (ordnance survey scale 1:1,250 is suitable, obtain copies from the applicant's surveyor);

(c) other plans and drawings needed to describe the proposed development – these will show, for example, elevation drawings, car parking arrangements, means of access and internal layout of the development (obtain copies from the applicant's architect);

(d) three additional copies of each of the above documents;

(e) certificate relating to ownership pursuant to s 65 (see below);

(f) appropriate planning fee – to determine the fee payable to the LPA, see Chapter 5.

The type of application which is needed depends on the nature of the proposal. The possibilities are:

(a) full planning permission;

(b) outline planning permission;

(c) application to approve the reserved matters left outstanding from a previous grant of outline planning permission;

(d) application to renew a previous temporary grant of planning permission;

(e) application to secure discharge or modification of a condition subject to which planning permission has previously been granted.

Although all such applications will be made on the same form, it is helpful to be able to specify the planning permission sought as this will aid the progress of the application. Most applications are for full planning permission, but in the case of development proposals involving construction of buildings, an outline application can be used to test the acceptability of the principle of development on the site in question without submitting full details of the development. Once it is accepted that a site can be 'released for development' the developer can obtain approval of the reserved matters at a later stage. In view of the possible need to appeal from the decision of the LPA, thus necessitating the use of more copies, it is advisable to obtain a dozen copies of each plan and drawing from the outset. This will ensure file copies are always available, ensure that copies are available for use in the event of an appeal and also cover the risk of accidental loss or damage.

No additional copies of the certificate of ownership referred to above need be submitted. The object of the certificate is to ensure that the applicant has notified other parties interested in the land, such as co-owners or a tenant who has a lease with at least seven years unexpired or who is an agricultural tenant. There are four possible certificates summarised as follows:

(a) *Certificate A* – the applicant owns all the land subject to the application;

(b) *Certificate B* – the applicant has notified those other persons who were owners 21 days before the date of the application;

(c) *Certificate C* – the applicant is not an owner of the land but has notified some of them and taken such steps as are reasonably open to him to identify other owners;

(d) *Certificate D* – the applicant is not an owner of the land and does not know who the owners are and has taken such steps as are reasonably open to him to identify them.

The form of each of these certificates is specified in Art 7 of and Sched 2, Pt 2 to the GDPO 1995. Most applications involve either Certificate A or Certificate B, examples of which are given in Chapter 7. All applications must be accompanied by a certificate otherwise the application cannot be entertained by the LPA. The certificate must also be correct as an applicant who knowingly submits a false certificate commits an offence under s 65(6) of the 1990 Act punishable by a maximum fine of £5,000.

The planning fee payable must be submitted with the application otherwise the LPA will treat the application as incomplete and can await payment of the fee before the application is decided. It is also necessary to submit the correct fee; if there is any doubt as to the sum payable contact the Planning Department of the LPA for clarification before submission is made. As to the relevant planning fee payable, see Chapter 5.

2.5.3 Post-submission

After submission, the LPA will acknowledge receipt in the form prescribed by Art 5 and Sched 1, Pt 1 to the GDPO 1995 and carry out notifications and consultations, for example, with other statutory authorities and also with neighbours. The planning officer dealing with the application may have powers delegated to him to decide the matter, though this will normally be confined to minor proposals or approval of reserved matters. In all other cases, the planning officer will draft a report to Committee which will detail the nature of the application, any relevant planning history, results of responses to consultations, details of any objections received and will conclude with a recommendation as to whether or not planning permission should be granted. If the recommendation is positive, the report to Committee will also contain details of any conditions which the planning officer recommends should be attached to the grant of planning permission. The report, together with similar reports relating to other applications, will be placed on the agenda for the Planning Committee meeting of the LPA which will decide the application. This recommendation is crucial as the Planning Committee will in most instances follow the advice of their officers. Since most LPAs do not advise applicants in writing when the relevant meeting of the Planning Committee will be held (unless the applicant or an objector has requested an opportunity to make oral representations at the relevant meeting), nor give advice of the recommended decision, it is necessary to contact the LPA to discover these details.

As a matter of routine you should always study the content if the planning officer's report to committee because:

(a) it may contain factual errors which, if not corrected, may mislead the Planning Committee;

(b) it may contain contentious application or interpretation of policy guidance which could be resolved by further discussion;

(c) reasons for recommending refusal may be relevant to only part of the proposed development, thereby indicating that a less ambitions scheme might be supported;

(d) it will normally be advisable to withdraw an application which is opposed by the relevant planning officer.

If an adverse recommendation has been made, it is desirable to obtain the reasons for the recommendation as it may be possible to revise the application in some respect, for example, a lower density of development, or persuade the planning officer to change his mind or withdraw one or more reasons for recommending refusal. This is particularly important if an appeal is contemplated as it is easier to appeal against a decision in respect of which two reasons have been given for refusal rather than three!

Even if the planning officer is recommending that planning permission should be granted, it is necessary to ensure that any conditions that are being recommended should be attached to the grant are acceptable to the developer.

2.5.4 Dealing with planning officers

When dealing with planning officers a useful approach is to discuss but not debate the planning merits of applications. Meetings should be used as opportunities to gather information rather than precipitate conclusions. Even if the relevant area planning officer appears to be unreasonably stubborn in opposing an application for planning permission which you consider merits approval, avoid engaging in debate, especially in front of clients. Although you will want to impress your client with your ability to 'deliver', a much more successful approach is to conduct discussions in a way which does not challenge reasons for opposition but seeks to evaluate the strength of them as some will be more significant than others. This is particularly important in instances where the development plan is not conclusive and the matter has to be resolved having regard to other material considerations. If the proposal could be modified, there may be a detectable change in attitude, as also may be the case if conditions attached to a potential grant can be successfully negotiated. Information gathered from such discussions enables you to form a considered view on:

(a) how the application could be modified to reduce or eliminate grounds of opposition;

(b) how to establish the principle of development on the relevant site;

(c) whether the application should be withdrawn and a different form of development considered;

(d) whether there are reasonably sound prospects of a successful appeal which would justify the risk of refusal of planning permission.

Remember also, that when the current matter has been determined the likelihood is that you will need to deal with the same planning officer on other occasions. Attempt therefore to build a relationship of mutual professional respect.

2.5.5 The Planning Committee meeting

The Planning Committee meets on a regular cycle, usually about every four weeks. Under s 1 of the Local Government (Access to Information) Act 1985, the meeting is held in public and copies of the agenda are made available for use by members of the public, applicants and their advisers. Whether you will be permitted to address the Committee depends on the standing orders of the LPA; practice in this respect varies. Where the opportunity is granted, it is often limited to a statement not exceeding five minutes. It is best to have a written prepared statement in order to succeed in making as many points as can be made in a limited time. These points must, in order to be effective, be planning considerations, as distinct from emotive ones. If you are permitted to address the meeting you should bear in mind that any objectors will be entitled to do so on natural justice principles: *R v Great Yarmouth BC ex p Battan Bros Arcades Ltd* (1987) 56 P & CR 99.

Although it will not necessarily be apparent at the meeting, the Planning Committee are required in making their decision to 'have regard to the provisions of the development plan, so far as material to the application, and to any other material considerations' (s 70 of the 1990 Act). It is useful to bear in mind (and to remind the Committee if you have the opportunity) that all applicants have a presumption in their favour that planning permission will be granted if the application is consistent with the provisions of the development plan. This is contained in PPG1 – *General Policies and Principles*, para 40 of which states that 'The Government is committed to a plan-led system of development control ... Where an adopted or approved development plan contains relevant policies, s 54A requires that an application for planning permission ... shall be determined in accordance with the plan unless material considerations indicate otherwise. Conversely, applications which are not in accordance with relevant policies in the plan should not be allowed unless material considerations justify granting a planning permission. Those deciding such applications ... should always take into account whether the proposed development would cause demonstrable harm to interests of acknowledged importance'. This statement of policy expressly takes into account the requirement enacted in s 54A of the 1990 Act, which specifies that 'any determinations under the Planning Acts ... shall be made in accordance with the plan unless material considerations indicate otherwise'.

The decision of the committee may be:

(a) to grant planning permission unconditionally;

(b) to grant planning permission subject to such conditions as they think fit;

(c) to refuse planning permission.

In some cases, the decision will be deferred to the next meeting, perhaps pending a site visit or receipt of further advice from the local highway authority (the county council). The LPA and the applicant must bear in mind, however, that if a decision is not reached within eight weeks of the submission of the application it is to be assumed that the application has been refused unless a longer period is agreed in writing (s 78(5) of the 1990 Act).

2.5.6 Subsequent to the meeting

Whatever the decision of the LPA, a written communication will be received. If planning permission is granted a document confirming that this is so will be issued. Where planning permission is granted subject to conditions, reasons will be given for the imposition of the conditions. Similarly, in the event that the application is not successful the LPA will issue a notice of refusal, in most instances faithfully reproducing the planning officer's draft of unwithdrawn reasons why he recommended that the application should be refused.

The LPA are required to state their reasons clearly and precisely. Following making of the Town and Country Planning (General Development Procedure) (Amendment) (England) Order 2000 SI 2000/1627, the LPA are also required to specify all the policies and proposals in the development plan which are relevant to the decision. A planning consent or a notice of refusal must be carefully retained, the former because of its relevance to a purchaser of the property, the latter because it is necessary to submit a copy on making an appeal against the decision of the LPA to the Secretary of State.

2.6 Application for a certificate of lawfulness of proposed use or development

2.6.1 Section 192 of the 1990 Act

Section 192 makes available the useful facility of applying to the LPA for a certificate whether or not a grant of planning permission is needed for a particular proposal. The application for a certificate of lawfulness of proposed use or development (known as a CLOPUD) requests the LPA to determine whether any proposed use or proposed operations would be lawful. It is only available prior to the carrying-out of a proposed act of development and hence is not available to determine the lawfulness of any development which has already been implemented. It is available in respect of all forms of development but is particularly appropriate to test whether a proposed change of use would constitute a material change of use, for example, if a doctor or other professional person proposes to use rooms in his house for consulting purposes, the rooms being available for his own use outside consulting hours. If a favourable determination is obtained this is as good as obtaining planning permission (*Wells v Minister of Housing and Local Government* (1967) 65 LGR 43) since the lawfulness of the proposed use or operations is 'conclusively presumed' (s 192(4)).

2.6.2 Preparation and submission of the application

Procedure in s 192 applications is as specified by Art 24 of the GDPO 1995, that is, that the application be in writing and contain a description of the proposal, the existing use of the land or the last use (including a reference, where appropriate, to the relevant use class specified in the Town and Country Planning (Use Classes) Order 1987), the reasons for regarding the proposed use as lawful, any other information which the applicant considers relevant, and appropriate plans. There is currently no prescribed form of application. In practice, this means that the application consists of:

(a) application form and three additional copies – this should be obtained by making a written request to the LPA;

(b) site plan;

(c) other plans and drawings needed to describe the proposed development – in change of use cases, a plan can sometimes be dispensed with but, since the applicant must give a full description of the proposed use, this will usually be facilitated by submission of a plan;

(d) statement of the applicant's interest in the land and whether there are any other parties known to the applicant and whether he has notified them of the making of the application;

(d) relevant planning fee – to determine the fee payable to the LPA, see Chapter 5.

Unlike a planning application, no additional copies of the form or plans are required to be submitted. LPA planning officers do not always remember, however, that Art 24 of the GDPO 1995 makes no mention of additional copies in s 192 cases and erroneously demand further copies before processing the application. This can lead to a delay and hence it is advisable to submit three extra copies from the outset; delay is more likely to lead to a deemed decision that planning permission is required.

Annexed to the form of application should be the description of the proposal. Using the example given above of a proposal by a medical practitioner to use rooms in a dwelling house for consulting purposes the description should be similar to the example given in Chapter 7.

2.6.3 Post-submission

An application for a determination under s 192 is unlikely to be discussed at a Planning Committee meeting as the question is ultimately one of law rather than policy. The decision (which must be issued within eight weeks of receipt of the application, unless a longer period is agreed in writing) will normally be made by a planning officer under delegated powers in consultation with a member of the council's legal department. It will be communicated by a formal document resembling a grant of planning permission. The form of the certificate, if granted, will be as specified in Sched 4 to the GDPO 1995.

2.7 Application for a certificate of lawfulness of existing use or development

2.7.1 Section 191 of the 1990 Act

Another very useful provision of the 1990 Act is s 191 which enables an application to be made for a certificate of lawfulness of existing use or development (known as a CLEUD). As the name implies, the object of obtaining such a certificate is to establish that an existing development is lawful and that it is therefore immune from enforcement proceedings. Such an application will only be applicable where a relevant grant of planing permission has not previously been obtained and the development in question was carried out in breach of planning control. Most importantly, the time for taking enforcement action by the LPA must have passed in accordance with the limitation periods specified in s 171B of the 1990 Act. In the case of operational development, this is four years calculated from the date on which the development is substantially completed; in the case of a material change of use, this is 10 years (other than a change of use to use as a single dwelling house in respect of which the relevant period is four years), time being calculated from the date of the breach. An additional benefit of using this procedure is that it establishes the planning title, thus, facilitating a future sale.

Implementation of the procedure will often take place when the LPA are considering enforcement action or have requested the applicant to make an application for planning permission in respect of the development which has already taken place. Where the available evidence shows that relevant time limit has passed, the better option may be to make an application for a CLEUD rather than seek a grant of planning permission. This is because the LPA have no power to attach conditions to a CLEUD.

2.7.2 Preparation and submission of the application

The procedural arrangements are the same as apply to a CLOPUD (see 2.6.2 above) in that although there is no prescribed form of application, Art 24 of the GDPO 1995 applies. The required contents of the application are therefore specified by that provision. If the application is successful the LPA will issue a certificate in the form prescribed by Sched 4 to the GDPO 1995.

Annex 8 of the Department of the Environment, Transport and the Regions Circular 10/97 *Enforcing Planning Control*, makes clear that the onus of proof lies on the applicant but the standard of proof is the balance of probability. If the evidence is sufficient to satisfy the LPA that the applicant has discharged the burden of proof a CLEUD must be issued (s 191(4)).

2.8   Application for listed building consent or conservation area consent

2.8.1   The Planning (Listed Buildings and Conservation Areas) Regulations 1990

These Regulations (SI 1990/1519, the '1990 Regulations') specify the requirements with which an applicant for either consent must comply. They are broadly similar to those imposed by the GDPO 1995 in relation to planning applications. They do not in any sense replace the requirements of the 1995 Order as in all cases in which 'development' is involved, both an application for planning permission and an application for listed building or conservation area consent must be made. The main areas of similarity are that:

(a) the applicant must submit a certificate relating to ownership in the prescribed form (see Chapter 7);

(b) the programme for dealing with the application is such that a decision should be notified to the applicant within eight weeks of submission of the application, unless a longer period is agreed in writing.

2.8.2   Preparation and submission of the application

In order to make an application for listed building or conservation area consent, reg 3 of the 1990 Regulations requires the following to be submitted:

(a) application form – this should be obtained by making a written request to the LPA (it is not a prescribed form);

(b) plans and drawings – the regulations do not expressly require submission of a plan to describe the proposed works, or a site plan, but it may be concluded that this is what is intended (scale 1:1,250 should be used);

(c) certificate relating to ownership.

A planning fee is not required as this type of application falls outside the scope of the planning fees regime (see Chapter 5). Guidance on the making of applications for listed building consent is contained in Annex B to PPG 15 (Planning and the Historic Environment). Paragraph B3 advises that the applicant must submit two additional copies of the form of application and the accompanying plans and drawings which describe the works for which consent is sought. These will normally include drawings of all relevant floor plans and external or internal elevations which will be affected by the proposed works. In addition, it is often particularly helpful to the LPA, and hence to the applicant, to submit photographs of the elevations where consent to demolish is sought or the affected part(s) of the buildings if alteration or extension is proposed.

2.8.3 Post-submission

On receipt of the submission the LPA will issue an acknowledgement in the form prescribed by Sched 1 to the 1990 Regulations. Thereafter, the LPA will take steps to advertise the making of the application by:

(a) placing an appropriate notice in a local newspaper giving details of the nature of the proposed works and stating that the application can be inspected during the next 21 days;

(b) posting a site notice on or near the building which must be in position for not less than seven days and contain the same information as the newspaper notification.

The application must not be determined before 21 days have elapsed from the newspaper notice and placing in position of the site notice, and any representations received must be taken into account in reaching the decision (reg 5). Exceptions from these publicity requirements apply, however, if the proposed works requiring listed building consent would affect only the interior of the building and its rating as a listed building is only Grade II. Thus, the publicity procedure applies to all works to buildings listed Grade I or Grade II*. The LPA will then proceed to determine the application taking into account representations received from persons, other than the applicant, who have been notified by him because of their status as owners. Listed building consent or conservation area consent can be granted unconditionally, or subject to conditions, or can be refused.

2.9 Opposing development proposals

2.9.1 Methods of opposition

An applicant for a grant of planning permission has a right of appeal under s 78 of the 1990 Act against refusal of the application or grant subject to conditions. A neighbour or other third party has no right of appeal and, hence, a disappointed objector is, subject to the possibility of judicial review, obliged to accept that the developer has been successful. In view of this it is essential that an unwelcome proposal by a developer is vigorously and effectively opposed at the application stage. Most clients seeking assistance in these circumstances will be local residents who have been notified of the making of the planning application by the LPA pursuant to notification requirements imposed by Art 8 of GDPO 1995 which requires the LPA to inform adjoining owners and occupiers or to display a site notice. The form of the notice is specified by Sched 3 to the Order. On receipt of such a notification it is essential to inspect the application itself by calling at the office of the LPA and examining the relevant entry in the planning register maintained under s 69 of the 1990 Act. It is helpful to look at all the entries in this register relating to the property to discover if similar proposals have previously been rejected and also to inspect the register of enforcement and stop notices to gain further information about the planning history of the site. You may even discover that the applicant has been in breach of planning control with a similar proposal, thus, enabling you to write an informed letter of objection to the LPA. Any such letter will need to be drafted to meet the needs of the client, but an example is given in Chapter 7.

Before writing to the LPA on behalf of your client, consider the provisions of the development plan with a view to identifying relevant policies to which you may be able to refer. Writing a suitable letter of objection is an effective means of opposition as the fact of the making of the objection will be recorded in the agenda for the Planning Committee and copies of your letter may be circulated. This should be treated as a routine step in opposition to a proposal but it should be followed up with political measures. The client should therefore be advised to:

(a) contact his local councillor with a view to persuading the councillor to speak against the proposal at the Planning Committee meeting and to encourage other members to do so;

(b) contact the parish council, if any, as the written views of the parish council submitted to the LPA will carry considerable weight;

(c) if the application is a very significant one, advise the client to contact the local MP with a view to asking him to attempt to persuade the Secretary of State to 'call-in' the application for his own decision under s 77. If this is done the Secretary of State will convene a public local inquiry before deciding the application;

(d) encourage neighbours and other persons resident in the area to take similar action.

2.9.2 Repeat applications

Even if a proposal is successfully opposed the client must be advised to be alert to the possibility that the developer may make a repeat application with a slightly modified proposal. A determined developer may seek to 'wear down' the opposition by such tactics since subsequent proposals are often less enthusiastically opposed, perhaps because objectors sometimes erroneously believe that having expressed objection once there is no need to do so again. This is a totally false belief and, moreover, the developer will often seek to argue the acceptability of his proposal by making specific reference to the lack of objections at both the application stage and (if necessary) on appeal to the Secretary of State.

Where a repeat application is made the LPA are empowered by s 70A of the 1990 Act to decline to determine it if they consider that the application is the same or substantially the same as a previous application which was refused by them or the Secretary of State not more than two years before the current application was made. In exercising this power, the LPA must be satisfied that there has been no significant change in the development plan, so far as material to the application, or in any other material considerations.

3 Challenges to Planning Decisions

As far as possible, all disputes which arise under the town and country planning legislation are resolved administratively rather than by recourse to the courts. Thus, s 78 of the Town and Country Planning Act 1990 (the '1990 Act') confers a right of appeal from the LPA to the Secretary of State on an applicant who:

(a) has been refused planning permission; or

(b) has been granted planning permission subject to conditions which he is unwilling to accept.

3.1 Planning appeals

3.1.1 Gathering information

The first consultation with the client may well take place only at the appeal stage, the applicant having previously made the application himself or with the assistance of an architect or surveyor. If you are being instructed at the appeal stage the first point to determine is whether the proposed appeal is out of time: under Art 23(2) of the Town and Country Planning (General Development Procedure) Order 1995 SI 1995/419, six months are allowed from the date of the LPA's decision in which to appeal to the Secretary of State. Article 23 was amended by Art 4 of the Town and Country Planning (General Development Procedure) (England) (Amendment) Order 2000 SI 2000/1627 which enables the Secretary of State to refuse to accept a notice of appeal unless all supporting documentation is submitted within the six-month period. There is nevertheless a discretion conferred on the Secretary of State to accept a late appeal (Art 23(2)).

If the proposed appeal is still in time, obtain from the client (or previous agent) the following documents:

(a) a copy of the application for planning permission;

(b) 12 copies of all plans and drawings;

(c) copies of all correspondence with the LPA;

(d) the relevant planning officer's report to committee;

(e) the decision of the LPA;

(f) a copy of the Art 6 notice and Art 7 certificate.

Study of these documents, the development plan, relevant departmental circulars, planning policy guidance, any applicable regional policy guidance, the site and its surroundings will enable you to form a preliminary conclusion as to whether it is worthwhile making an appeal. If the application was one which was doomed to failure from the outset there is little point in pursuing the matter to appeal and the client should be advised accordingly. If, however, there appear to be good grounds for arguing that the proposal is consistent with the policies of the development plan, complies with departmental policy guidance, and that on the planning merits planning permission should be granted, it will be necessary to build up further knowledge of the planning issues and of the site in order to prepare the appeal. This can be achieved by:

(a) searching in the register of planning applications and decisions maintained by the LPA under s 69 of the 1990 Act in relation to the appeal site and nearby premises. From this search it will be possible to discover the attitude displayed by the LPA to any previous proposals for development, for example, if a similar proposal affecting nearby property has succeeded, and, in particular, whether the Secretary of State has issued any planning appeal decisions relevant to the site or nearby premises. Search is by personal attendance at the LPA's offices. No fee is payable;

(b) obtaining from the LPA copies of any 'background papers' relevant to the decision, for example, supplementary planning guidance, responses from consultees in respect of the application, letters of objection or of support for the proposed development. These will normally be recorded in the planning officer's report to committee;

(c) studying the results of a recent search of the local land charges register and replies to Enquiries of the Local Authority or requisitioning new searches.

3.1.2 The method of appeal

Under s 79(2) of the 1990 Act both the appellant and the LPA have a right to appear before and be heard by a 'person appointed' by the

Secretary of State before the appeal is determined. If either party insists on this facility, the Secretary of State will either arrange a hearing or convene a public local inquiry under s 320 of the 1990 Act. The Secretary of State has advised on issue of Department of the Environment, Transport and the Regions (DETR) Circular 05/2000 *Planning Appeals: Procedures* that hearings are to be preferred rather than public inquiries. This change may prove beneficial to both appellants and to the efficient administration of the appeal system, as there are clear advantages in promoting the use of hearings rather than inquiries. Public inquiries are, however, notoriously expensive and even if likely to last only one day they are commonly avoided in favour of resolution of the appeal by alternative methods.

Although, a public inquiry will continue to be appropriate in cases where the financial advantages of a successful appeal are large compared to the cost of the inquiry, or where the arguments to be advanced address complex planning issues which require oral rather than written evidence and involve the calling of expert witnesses and cross-examination of the LPA's witnesses, the alternative of a hearing will seem attractive in many instances. Comparatively little use was made of hearings prior to the change of policy announced in DETR Circular 05/2000 and the great majority (about 85%) of planning appeals were decided following the submission of written representations to the Secretary of State. While most appeals will continue to be resolved using the written representations procedure, now regulated by the Town and Country Planning (Appeals) (Written Representations Procedure) Regulations 2000 SI 2000/1628, many appellants will seek a hearing where they may have previously been less inclined to seek a public inquiry. The change in emphasis in favour of hearings is underlined by the making of the Town and Country Planning (Hearings Procedure) (England) Rules 2000 SI 2000/1626, hearings having been previously been conducted pursuant to an informal code contained in Annex 2 to Department of the Environment (DoE) Circular 2/88.

3.1.3 Preparing the appeal

Planning appeals are made on a form obtainable from the DETR. In addition to several copies of this form, appellants are supplied by the Department with certificates relating to ownership of the land, one of which will be relevant and will have to be submitted with the appeal. Also, the Departmental booklet *Planning Appeals – A Guide to Procedure* will be enclosed. Study the guide carefully before attempting to complete the appeal form. Although the form is intelligently devised, it is nevertheless a complex one; to avoid errors on the final draft, make a photocopy of it first and fill in the photocopy. Apart from the points of factual detail sought by the form, space is made available on the form for stating the 'grounds of appeal'. This is of course the critical part of the submission and considerable skill is needed in drafting the grounds in such a way that the LPA's reasons for refusal of planning permission are shown to be unsatisfactory. Quite how this is to be achieved is, in part, a matter of experience, as well as knowledge of planning law, policy and practice. Most appeals do not raise difficult points of law as the dispute is usually over the application of planning policy at local and national level and the merits of the case. Hence a sophisticated knowledge of planning law is not essential. It is advisable to be concise (extra pages can be used if you feel that the argument warrants it) and strictly relevant to the issue.

Examine each reason for refusal given by the LPA in turn, splitting them up into sections if necessary, to facilitate analysis and point out the weaknesses. The structure of the draft can be given sub-headings as the case dictates, for example, a short introduction giving a site description and brief planing history, and then the argument on relevant development plan policies and objectives and the planning merits (this is the main part of the submission), and finally, a conclusion. It is very important to use 'planning language' in the draft to convey the impression that your case has been properly prepared and that you thereby make your points confidently. It is, therefore, prudent to use the words used in the 1990 Act, subordinate legislation and policy documents, for example, 'highway' rather than 'road' or 'street', 'dwelling house' rather than 'house', 'amenity' rather than 'pleasant circumstances', etc. One way of acquiring familiarity with the terms to be used is to read decision letters issued in relation to previous planning appeals, particularly if relevant to the area of the site. These can be inspected at the offices of the LPA but it will normally be necessary to obtain photocopies, for which a charge will be made. Consultation of such letters also provides a helpful guide to the structure of the draft grounds of appeal.

An example of the use of the planning appeal form is given below. In the hypothetical application leading to the appeal, the applicant sought to obtain planning permission to change the use of a retail shop to use as an estate agent's office. The application has been refused by Worktown District Council for the reasons which have been reproduced in the 'grounds of appeal' section of the form.

Planning Appeal to the Secretary of State: Town and Country Planning Act 1990 and Town and Country Planning (General Development Procedure) Order 1995

Please complete this form clearly and send one copy to the Inspectorate and one copy to the local planning authority.

A Information about the appellant(s)

(1) Full name(s) *Arthur Brian Client*

(2) Address *29 Hall Lane, Worktown, Planshire, Postcode WT7 3PR*

Daytime telephone number *Worktown 337365*

Reference –

(3) Agent's name (if any) *AN Other & Co, Solicitors*

(4) Agent's address *14 Union Street, Worktown, Planshire, Postcode WT1 2BG*

Daytime telephone number *Worktown 342848*

Reference *ANO/AB/CLIENT*

B Details of the appeal

(5) Name of local planning authority (LPA) *Worktown District Council*

(6) Description of the development: *Change of use from shop for the sale of retail goods (Use Class A1) and ancillary first floor storage use, to use as office premises for the purposes of estate agency (Use Class A2).*

(7) (a) Address of the site: *44 Sebastopol Street, Worktown*

(b) National Grid reference (see key on Ordnance Survey Map for instructions). Grid letters: *TQ* Grid numbers: *437725*

(8) Date and reference number of application against which you are appealing: 14 January 2001 Ref W/APP/2001/672

(9) Date of decision (if any): *8 March 2001*

C Procedure

(10) Do you agree to the written procedure (ie, an exchange of written statements with the LPA plus a visit to the site by a Planning Inspector)? Yes/No

OR

Do you wish to appear before, and be heard by, an Inspector (ie a local inquiry or hearing)? Yes/No

If you agree to the written procedure, could the Inspector see the whole site clearly from the road or other public land? Yes/No

D Supporting documents

You must enclose a copy of each of the following with the appeal form sent to the Inspectorate:

- the application made to the local planning authority;

- any Art 6 certificate submitted to the local planning authority;

- the appropriate Art 7 certificate for this appeal (look at the Notes then tick a box to show which certificate you have enclosed). It is important that you also enclose a copy of the Notice if you have completed Certificate B, C or D:

   A ☐   B ☐   C ☐   D ☐   Notice ☐

- each of the plans, drawings and documents sent to the LPA as part of the application they considered;

- the LPA's decision (if any);

- all other relevant correspondence with the LPA;

- a plan showing the site, marked in red, in relation to two named roads (preferably on an extract from the relevant 1:10,000 OS Map).

You should also enclose copies of the following, if appropriate:

- any notice and the appropriate certificate provided to the LPA in accordance with s 65 of the Act;

- if the appeal concerns reserved matters, the relevant outline application, plans submitted and the permission;

- any other plans, drawings and documents sent to the LPA but which did not form part of the application (eg, drawings for illustrative purposes);

- any additional plans or drawings relating to the application but not previously seen by the LPA. Number them clearly and note the numbers here.

E The appeal

This appeal is against the decision of the LPA:

(1) refusing/granting subject to conditions, planning permission for the development described above;

(2) refusing/granting subject to conditions, approval of the matters reserved under an outline planning permission;

(3) refusing to approve any matter (other than those mentioned in (2) above) required by a condition on a planning permission; (OR)

(4) the failure of the LPA to give notice of their decision within the appropriate period on an application for permission or approval.

F Grounds of appeal

If you have agreed to the written procedure you must make your full statement of case here; if you do not your appeal may be invalid. If you have not agreed to the written procedure, you should give a brief outline of your case.

Introductory

(1) The appeal premises comprise a ground floor retail shop with ancillary storage accommodation on the first floor. They are situated at the end of a small terrace of property comprising four units fronting onto Sebastopol Street between the All Saints' Church and North Street. Opposite the appeal premises there is a Fire Station and a public house. To the rear the property is served by Bank Street which also gives access to a municipal car park. Immediately adjacent to the appeal premises is 46 Sebastopol Street which is in use as an insurance agent's office.

The planning merits

(2) The LPA refused planning permission on two grounds. The first of these concerns the loss of a ground floor shopping facility. They state in the Notice of Refusal that:

> *'The proposed change of use from retail shop (Use Class A1) to use for office purposes (Use Class A2) would result in the loss of a ground floor shopping facility within the length of this important retail frontage and in the opinion of the Local Planning Authority the intrusion of a ground floor office use at this point is undesirable and conflicts with Policy s 8 of the Worktown Local Plan which generally prohibits such changes of use.'*

There are three elements in this statement:

(a) 'The proposal would result in the loss of a ground floor shopping facility within the length of this important retail frontage.' This part of the ground is based on the view that the appeal premises are comprised in an 'important retail frontage'. Having regard to the situation of the appeal premises in Sebastopol Street (as described above) it is submitted that the contribution of the appeal premises is minor and that they can be released for the proposed change of use without detriment to the remaining (more important) lengths of Sebastopol Street.

(b) The LPA state that 'the intrusion of a ground floor office use at this point is undesirable'. Here the LPA appear to claim that the proposed use is in some way novel thus creating the 'intrusion'. It is clear that since the adjacent premises are in current use as an insurance agent's office the proposed use of the appeal premises would not create an intrusion but merely emulate an existing neighbouring use.

(c) The LPA state that the proposal 'conflicts with Policy S 8'. The relevant paragraph of the Worktown Local Plan (adopted 17/4/97) provides that 'Within the frontages defined in the local plan ... the change to office use of (i) ground floor premises in shopping frontages ... will be resisted'. While it may be inferred that the purpose of this policy is to preserve retail characteristics, it is submitted that an estate agency, rather than being exclusively an office use, has characteristics in common with shops and hence such a use does not represent a significant departure from Policy S 8. Indeed, the Secretary of State has advised in Pt 2 of Planning Policy Guidance Note 6 (Town Centres and Retail Developments) that 'the vitality and viability of town centres depend on a number of factors including retaining and developing a wide range of attractions and facilities. In exercising their planning powers, local authorities are advised by para 2.12 of PPG 6 that they should encourage diversification of uses in the town centre as a whole'. If planning permission is granted for the proposed use a suitable planning condition could, however, be attached to the grant preventing the use of the premises for other uses in Class A2 of the Schedule to the Town and Country Planning (Use Classes) Order 1987.

(3) The second ground of refusal concerns staff parking provision. The LPA states that:

> Staff parking provision cannot be made available within the site to the likely detriment of parking provision for shoppers in this vicinity.

There are two elements in this statement:

(a) The assertion that 'staff parking provision cannot be made available within the site'. This is incorrect. At present the rear of the appeal premises consists of an area of former garden, now in unkempt condition upon which some rubbish has gathered. The dimensions of this area are approximately 20 feet wide by 70 feet in depth (1,400 square feet). Suitable surfacing of the rear part of the appeal premises will provide a car parking facility for staff cars. It may be noted on inspection that the rear of the adjacent premises (46 Sebastopol Street) is used for staff car parking and that the dimensions of the rear area are very similar to those of the rear of the appeal premises. The inference that the rear of the appeal premises could be used for parking provision is therefore impossible to resist. To overcome this ground of refusal of planning permission the appellant is willing to accept planning conditions requiring the hard surfacing of the rear area to the satisfaction of the LPA, and approval by the LPA of the parking arrangement.

(b) The LPA also assert that staff parking provision (if not available on-site) would be 'to the likely detriment of parking provision for shoppers *in this vicinity'. The LPA therefore concedes the availability of off-site parking facilities. They rely on the proposition that the use of the facilities would be detrimental to shoppers. Some 350 spaces are available in municipal car parks near the appeal premises. Supplementary Planning Guidance: Car Parking Standards issued by the LPA in 1997 makes it clear that the proposed change of use requires provision of fewer overall spaces than does the existing shop use. This would therefore have the effect of increasing the number of spaces available for other users of the town centre parking facilities.*

(4) For the above reasons the appellant respectfully requests that this appeal be allowed.

COMPLETE AND SIGN THE DECLARATION BELOW.

I confirm that a copy of each of the supporting documents indicated above is enclosed and that the relevant plans have been clearly marked.

I also confirm that a copy of this appeal form and any supporting documents not previously seen by the LPA has been sent to them.

Signed (on behalf of) *Arthur Brian Client*

Name (in capitals) *AN Other & Co Solicitors*

Now check that you have:

(a) completed the form;

(b) enclosed all the supporting documents;

(c) set out above the full grounds of appeal.

Send one copy of the appeal form with all the supporting documents to:

> The Planning Inspectorate
> DETR
> Tollgate House
> Houlton Street
> Bristol BS2 9DJ

The second copy of the appeal form must be sent to the LPA at the address from which you received the decision on your application (or any acknowledgments, etc) enclosing only copies of those documents not previously seen by the LPA.

Note: in instances where the appellant's grounds of appeal are not set out or not fully set out in the appeal form but are submitted at a later date in accordance with the Town and Country Planning (Appeals) (Written Representations Procedure) (England) Regulations 2000, guidance on the format of the written statement is contained in Annex 1(i) to DETR Circular 05/2000 *Planning*

Appeals: Procedures. In summary, this advises appellants to: (1) always cite the appeal reference number; (2) give a description of the site, location of the proposed development, the application for planning permission together with any revisions or amendments; (3) a concise statement of development plan policies which are material to the appeal, giving the status of all plans referred to (a copy of the title page will suffice for this purpose); (4) extracts from, or copies of, both the text and the written justification contained in the relevant policies should be set out in an appendix; (5) contents of PPGs and Circulars need only refer to the relevant paragraph numbers unless it is essential to make reference to the text; (6) a detailed history of the application should be avoided where this is not relevant to the appeal; (7) comments of persons (other than the parties) in support of the case and any references to planning appeal decisions should be set out in an appendix.

3.1.4 Submission checklist

Having drafted the grounds of appeal you will need to have two copies of the appeal form prepared. One copy will be submitted to the Planning Inspectorate and the other to the LPA. A considerable amount of documentation accompanies the submission to the Planning Inspectorate, but in the case of the LPA, only the appeal form need be sent together with any other plans or documents not previously submitted and which are contained in the appeal documentation.

Send the following documents with a covering letter listing the enclosures to the Planning Inspectorate, DETR, Tollgate House, Houlton Street, Bristol BS2 9DJ:

(a) appeal form (with any supplementary pages);

(b) copy application for planning permission, including plans and drawings (only one copy is required);

(c) copy of Art 7 certificate which accompanied the application for planning permission (see 2.5.2 for comment on this requirement);

(d) Art 7 certificate appropriate for this appeal;

(e) copy of site plan edged red, scale 1:10,000 identifying the land by reference to two named highways;

(f) copy of notice of refusal of planning permission issued by the LPA;

(g) copies of all correspondence with the LPA;

(h) copies of any documents referred to in the grounds of appeal (other than development plans), for example, relevant planning appeal decisions.

No planning fee is payable on making an appeal to the Secretary of State against refusal of planning permission or a grant subject to conditions. In certain cases, however, some supplementary documents will be needed in addition to those listed above, for example, copies of any plans or drawings which were sent to the LPA for illustrative purposes not forming part of the application for planning permission.

3.1.5 Post-submission

Acknowledgement of the appeal will be sent by the Planning Inspectorate by letter which will contain the following information:

(a) the appeal reference number;

(b) the room number of the Planning Inspectorate's case officer;

(c) the 'starting date' for the purposes of the Town and Country Planning (Appeals) (Written Representations Procedure) (England) Regulations 2000, if the appellant requested this procedure in the appeal form.

The Planning Inspectorate will send a similar letter to the LPA and a questionnaire to be completed and returned within two weeks. A copy will be received direct from the LPA. This is a lengthy document which elicits information about the nature of the property and the submissions of the LPA.

Within six weeks of the starting date, both the LPA and the appellant will submit detailed representations. A further three weeks are available to each party to comment on the other's written representations. Following an unaccompanied site visit (unless the inspector cannot view the site without entry) the inspector appointed to decide the appeal will issue a decision letter containing the reasons for the decision. The full timetable applicable to written representations appeals under the Town and Country Planning (Appeals) (Written Representations Procedure) (England) Regulations 2000 is set out in 4.2.1.

3.1.6 Informal hearing

If either the appellant or the LPA are unwilling to use the written representations method of appeal then appearance before a 'person appointed' (an inspector) will take place, either through the medium of a public local inquiry or through an informal hearing. The presumption is that the latter method will be used but the decision to convene a hearing rather than a public inquiry is a matter for the

Secretary of State rather than the parties. DETR Circular 05/2000 *Planning Appeals: Procedures* points out that the hearings procedure is simpler and quicker than the inquiries procedure and has the advantages that the parties can present their respective cases fully and fairly in a more relaxed and less formal atmosphere than at an inquiry. Appearance at a hearing is in the form of a round-the-table discussion led by the inspector. There is no cross-examination of witnesses unless the inspector considers it necessary to ensure a thorough examination of the main issues. The procedure is regulated by the Town and Country Planning (Hearings Procedure) (England) Rules 2000 SI 2000/1626 which seek to ensure that the inspector is fully appraised of the relevant issues and arguments before the hearing opens so that he is in a position to lead the discussion.

After submission of a valid appeal, the Secretary of State will specify a starting date, an appeal reference number and the address for communications to the Secretary of State.

The central feature of the hearings procedure is the preparation of the hearing statement. Two copies of this document should be submitted to the Secretary of State within six weeks of the starting date containing the full particulars of the appellant's case, together with copies of the documents to which reference is to be made at the hearing. One copy will be forwarded by the Secretary of State to the LPA, which should also submit a hearing statement within six weeks of the starting date. Both parties have the opportunity of commenting on the other's hearing statement within nine weeks of the starting date. The hearing date itself should be arranged to take place not later than 12 weeks after the starting date.

A recommended format for a hearing statement is contained in Annex 2(i) of DETR Circular 05/2000. This advises that, in addition to preparation of the case for each party, the appellants and the LPA are expected to submit a short summary of the evidence on which they can agree; this can be annexed to the main statement. The main body of the statement should set out the key facts, reasoning and conclusions necessary to make the appellant's case; expert opinions should also be stated and substantiated. Opinions on matters of subjective judgment should be kept brief but should be adequately explained. The statement should also contain suggested conditions which the appellant is willing to accept in the event that planning permission is granted by the Secretary of State.

Appendices should be presented within an A4 size binder; if more than one document is being referred to an index should be included. For ease of reference each page should be numbered and the binder should be capable of being laid flat. Plans are folded to be of A4 size and each placed in a transparent plastic wallet. Where photographs are used these are mounted on A4 size card and prefaced by a plan showing the viewpoints from which they were taken. The date and time on which they were taken and the focal length of the lens used should also be specified.

The hearing itself will be conducted in accommodation in which the parties can be seated round a table. This will usually mean use of a committee room rather than the council chamber. Although the procedure will be determined by the inspector, he will summarise his understanding of the case and the main issues. Although the Circular advises that legal representation 'should not normally be necessary', it is unlikely that the appeal will be conducted by the appellant without professional assistance; as with appeals resolved by other methods that role can be fulfilled by the appellant's solicitor.

In appropriate instances, submissions in respect of costs should be made at the conclusion of the hearing.

3.1.7 Public local inquiry

In those cases in which the appeal is to be determined following a public local inquiry, the procedure is regulated by the Town and Country Planning (Inquiries Procedure) (England) Rules 2000 SI 2000/1624 or (in the vast majority of such cases) by the Town and Country Planning (Determination by Inspectors) (Inquiries Procedure) (England) Rules 2000 (the '2000 Rules') SI 2000/1625. These Rules govern procedure applied during the pre-inquiry, inquiry, and post-inquiry stages and (*inter alia*) each contain a time table for a number of procedural matters. This timetable is set out in para 4.2.3.

Where the appellant considers from the outset of the appeal that the written representations procedure or a hearing is not suitable for resolving the appeal (as the issues are too complex requiring detailed examination of the evidence and cross-examination of LPA witnesses) the initial appeal documentation submitted to the Planning Inspectorate will, nevertheless, be very similar. Whether an inquiry is to be held, however, will be determined by the Planning Inspectorate, acting on behalf of the Secretary of State taking into account the circumstances of the appeal and the preferences expressed by the parties. The same appeal form is used though it is not essential to give a full account of the case in the grounds of appeal. It is sufficient to specify all the points of the appellant's case but without giving a detailed account of points to be made in support since to do so would pre-empt the object of participation in a public local inquiry. It must be borne in mind, however, that the case needs to be adequately described.

Where a public local inquiry is to take place the procedure is subject to a timetable linked to the 'relevant date'. This is the date of a written notice issued by the Secretary of State informing the parties that an inquiry will be held. The order of events leading up to the inquiry is explained in Chapter 4, but the central feature is that the appellant and the LPA will each prepare a 'statement of case' and submit two copies to the Secretary of State within six weeks of the starting date. The Secretary of State will then send a copy of each party's statement of case to the other party.

The statement of case is a written statement containing full particulars of the case which it is proposed to put forward at the inquiry including a list of any documents which are to be put in evidence. The inquiry itself will normally be held within 20 weeks of the starting date.

Evidence at the inquiry is given orally; each expert witness will normally read a summary of their evidence. Under the 2000 Rules, a summary is required when the main proof of evidence exceeds 1,500 words; this should normally be about one-10th of the length of the proof. Copies of both documents are served on the Planning Inspectorate by the respective parties at least four weeks before the inquiry date.

The object of reading a summary of the witness's proof of evidence is to save time at the inquiry. Any documents which are given in evidence can be appended to the main proof of evidence or, if very substantial, bound separately. Both the proofs, the summaries and other documents should not only make out the appellant's case but should also be clear and logical if they are to be found convincing. While these may well be considered points of common sense, a little experience is all that is necessary in order to appreciate how essential it is to achieve a high standard of drafting.

It must be noted that although inquiry procedure is regulated by procedural rules, these are not comprehensive and the inspector is given a general power to determine the procedure to be followed.

In addition to submission of a statement of case, proofs of evidence and summaries, the parties are required to submit to the Secretary of State an agreed statement of common ground. The object of this requirement is explained at Annex 3(ii) of DETR Circular 05/2000 which advises that agreed factual information about the proposal shortens the length of proofs of evidence. In many instances the statement of common ground will be relatively brief since it should be restricted to matters of fact and should not contain any opinion or comment. It will therefore include the description of the site, the precise nature of the proposed development, the planning history and the relevant policies. In cases where technical evidence fall to be considered, there may be common ground in relation to matters such as traffic flow data, design standards, and land availability. The statement of common ground is to be prepared jointly by the parties to the appeal and they are jointly responsible for submission to the Secretary of State at least four weeks before the inquiry commences.

Under the 2000 Rules, the order in which evidence is normally given has been reversed. The LPA will normally present their case first, the object of this change being to focus the inquiry on the main issues. The appellant will then be heard followed third parties who were required to be informed of the original planning application, and finally other persons without a legal interest. All but the last group can call witnesses and cross-examine witness who give evidence for other parties. The final group will be permitted to do this only in so far as the inspector may permit. Opening and closing submissions will also normally be made by the main parties.

The decision letter issued by the inspector will be sent to the appellant, the LPA, the third parties who were required to be informed of the original planning application and any other third parties who gave evidence and have requested to be notified of the decision. An earlier indication of what the decision is likely to be can be obtained, however, if all parties agree to request an 'advance notification of decision' from the inspector. If this is required the inspector will state the probable result after the inquiry has closed. Such notification is strictly non-statutory and the parties should therefore await the formal decision letter.

After the evidence to be given at the inquiry has been presented, the inspector will hear submissions in respect of the costs of the parties. See, further, Chapter 6.

3.2 Judicial review

3.2.1 Relevance of judicial review

So far this chapter has been concerned with planning appeal procedures which enable appellants to place in issue the merits of a decision made by the LPA. In all but a small minority of cases, this will be all that is needed. Those cases in which the question of judicial review arises concern grants of planning permission subject to conditions which the applicant considers *ultra vires*. Judicial review is, therefore, sought under RSC Ord 53 and s 31 of the Supreme Court Act 1981 (see Pt 50 of and Sched 1 to the Civil Procedure Rules 1998 (CPR)). For examples of cases appropriate for this procedure, see *Hall v Shoreham-by-Sea UDC* [1964] 1 All ER 1, *R v Hillingdon LBC ex p Royco Homes Ltd* [1974] 2 QB 720 and *Newbury DC v Secretary of State for the Environment* [1981] AC 578.

3.2.2 Application for judicial review

Leave of the High Court must be obtained in order to seek judicial review and the application must be made promptly and in any event not later than three months from the decision of the LPA unless the court considers that there is good reason for extending the period. The application for leave is made *ex parte* to a judge by means of filing in the Crown Office an application notice in Form 86A and written evidence verifying the facts relied on. The application notice is required to contain a statement of:

(a) the name and description of the applicant;

(b) the relief sought and the grounds upon which it is sought;

(c) the name and address of the applicant's solicitors;

(d) the applicant's address for service.

The application is normally determined by the judge without a hearing unless the applicant has requested to be heard. If leave is refused it is possible to renew the application after giving notice of intention to do so in Form 86B within 10 days of notification of the refusal; the renewed application will come before a judge sitting in open court.

If leave is granted, the application for judicial review is made by claim form in Form 86 (see CPR, Pt 4 and Practice Direction 4).

If a successful application for judicial review is made in respect of planning conditions which are alleged to be *ultra vires*, the normal result is that the High Court will grant the remedy of certiorari to quash the conditions. In so doing, it does not substitute new conditions; in some cases the whole grant of planning permission may have to be quashed because it cannot be left in force shorn of the invalid conditions, see, for example, *Kent CC v Kingsway Investments Ltd* [1971] AC 72. This possible result must, therefore, be borne in mind and in some cases the developer may need to be advised not to seek judicial review and to accept the conditions imposed. Similar considerations also apply to the making of a s 78 appeal to the Secretary of State against the imposition of planning conditions: on making an appeal the whole application is reconsidered by the

Secretary of State and this may result in a refusal of planning permission because the Secretary of State decides not to make an unconditional grant. In such cases, it is more appropriate to make a further application to the LPA under s 73 to discharge or modify the conditions; if the application is refused by the LPA the subsequent appeal to the Secretary of State will be confined to the issues arising from the imposition of the conditions without placing the initial grant of planning permission at risk.

3.3   Appeal from Secretary of State to the High Court

Once the Secretary of State has made a decision on an appeal to him under s 78, his decision is 'final' in accordance with s 79(5) of the 1990 Act. This means that no further challenge can be made on the merits of the decision. A challenge can be made, however, under s 288 in respect of matters which closely resemble the issues raised in judicial review proceedings. The section permits a 'person aggrieved' by the Secretary of State's decision to apply to the High Court within six weeks of his decision in order to have the decision quashed on the grounds that the Secretary of State has exceeded his powers or that any relevant requirements have not been complied with in reaching the decision and the applicant's interests have been substantially prejudiced by such non-compliance. The section is a complex one and has generated a substantial body of case law which defines its scope. Reference should be made to the standard planning law texts (see Chapter 10, 'Further Reading') for guidance on the meaning of 'person aggrieved', 'relevant requirements' and 'substantially prejudiced'. An application under this section is made using a Pt 8 claim form which must state the grounds of the application (CPR, Pt 8, Practice Direction 8B and RSC Ord 94, r 1(2)).

3.4   Enforcement appeals

3.4.1 Issue of enforcement notice

The LPA have a discretionary power to take enforcement action by way of issue and service of copies of an enforcement notice under s 172(1) in circumstances where a breach of planning control has occurred. Such a notice will require the breach of planning control to be remedied or to require the remedying of any injury to amenity which has been caused by the breach. Service is regulated by s 172(2)(3) which provides that:

(1) A copy of an enforcement notice shall be served:

    (a) on the owner and on the occupier of the land to which it relates; and

    (b) on any other person having an interest in that land, being an interest which, in the opinion of the authority, is materially affected by the notice.

(2) The service of the notice shall take place:

    (a) not more than 28 days after its date of issue; and

    (b) not less than 28 days before the date specified in it as the date on which it is to take effect.

The effect of these provisions is therefore that:

(a) the LPA have a maximum of 28 days in which to serve copies of the enforcement notice;

(b) a minimum period of 28 days must be allowed by the notice before it is to come into effect.

The latter period is critical because it is only during this period that an appeal against the enforcement notice can be made. The content of the notice requires careful study because it must comply with the requirements of s 173 and the Town and Country Planning (Enforcement Notices and Appeals) Regulations 1991 (the '1991 Regulations') SI 1991/2804. The notice must not only require the breach of planning control to be remedied but must also specify the following:

(a) the matters which appear to the LPA to constitute a breach of planning control (s 173(1)(a));

(b) whether the alleged breach of planning control consists of carrying-out development without planning permission or failure to comply with a condition or limitation subject to which planning permission has been granted (s 173(1)(b));

(c) the steps required by the LPA to be taken or the activities which the authority require to cease in order to remedy the breach (s 173(3));

(d) the period within which any step specified in the notice by the LPA is to be taken (different periods may be allowed for different steps) (s 173(9));

(e) the reasons why the local planning authority consider it expedient to issue the notice (s 173(10) and reg 3(a) of the 1991 Regulations);

(f) the precise boundaries of the land to which the notice relates, whether by reference to a plan or otherwise (s 173(10) and reg 3(b) of the 1991 Regulations);

(g) the date on which the notice is to come into effect (s 173(8)).

A notice which fails to specify all these matters may be a nullity and, therefore have no legal effect. The test is whether the notice tells the recipient 'fairly what he has done wrong and what he must do to remedy it'. One which fails to satisfy this test is 'so much waste paper' (*per* Upjohn LJ in *Miller-Mead v Minister of Housing and Local Government* [1963] 2 QB 196). A suspected nullity should, nevertheless, be the subject of an appeal to the Secretary of State.

A further primary consideration in enforcement proceedings is whether the issue of the enforcement notice is out of time. A four-year limitation period is imposed by s 171B(1) in respect of development of an 'operational' nature, while a 10-year limitation period applies to unauthorised material changes of use, with the sole exception of change of use of a building to use as a single dwelling house (which is subject to the four-year limitation period). All breaches of planning control which consist of failure to comply with a condition or limitation attached to a grant of planning permission are subject to a limitation period of 10 years (s 171B(3)).

Where the limitation period applies and has been exceeded the effect is that the notice is invalid. Nevertheless, the issue of the enforcement notice must be challenged by way of appeal to the Secretary of State. This is because if a prosecution of the developer does take place he is precluded by s 285 of the 1990 Act from raising the validity of the enforcement notice in his defence if he could have appealed to the Secretary of State on the same ground (*R v Smith (Thomas George)* (1984) 48 P & CR 392).

The enforcement notice will be accompanied by an explanatory note about enforcement appeal procedure. This will be in the form of a DETR booklet *Enforcement Notice Appeals – A Guide to Procedure*. The LPA should also issue a copy of the official appeal Form DoE 14069 and a further copy of the enforcement notice. The additional copy will be needed if the right of appeal to the Secretary of State is exercised.

3.4.2 The right of appeal

A right of appeal against an enforcement notice is available under s 174. The grounds of appeal are set out in s 174(2):

(a) that planning permission ought to be granted in respect of any breach of planning control which may be constituted by the matters stated in the notice, or, as the case may be, that a condition or limitation alleged in the enforcement notice not to have been complied with ought to be discharged;

(b) that those matters have not taken place;

(c) that those matters (if they occurred) do not constitute a breach of planning control;

(d) that, at the date when the notice was issued, no enforcement action could be taken in respect of any breach of planning control which may be constituted by those matters;

(e) that copies of the enforcement notice were not served as required by s 172;

(f) that the steps required by the notice to be taken exceed what is necessary to remedy any breach of planning control which may be constituted by those matters or to remedy any injury to amenity which has been caused by any such breach;

(g) that the period specified in the notice as the period within which any step is to be taken falls short of what should reasonably be allowed.

One or more of these grounds may be relevant to the appeal and will be specified accordingly on completion of Form 14069. The most important consideration is, however, the need to submit notice of appeal to the Secretary of State within the limited time available: the key date is the day before that which is specified in the enforcement notice itself as the date on which the notice is to come into effect. The latter date will be a minimum of 28 days from the date on which the copy of the enforcement notice is served. The appeal must be made in time as the Secretary of State has no jurisdiction to entertain an appeal which is out of time (*Howard v Secretary of State for the Environment* [1975] 1 QB 235). Particular regard must be paid to the decision in *Lenlyn Ltd v Secretary of State for the Environment* (1984) JPL 482, in which it was held that notice of appeal must be received by the Secretary of State before the specified date and that it is not sufficient if the appeal documents arrive on that day. Note, however, should be made of s 174(3) which provides that an appeal can be made either (a) by giving written notice of the appeal to the Secretary of State before the date specified in the enforcement notice, or (b) by sending written notice of the appeal in a properly addressed and pre-paid letter posted to him at such time that in the ordinary course of post it would be delivered to him before that date.

If instructions are received at a late stage it is sufficient to send a letter to the Planning Inspectorate simply stating that you wish to appeal against the enforcement notice giving brief details of the land, the appellant, and the LPA. Further details of the appeal ie the grounds and the facts on which reliance will be placed, can be submitted later following a request on that behalf by the Secretary of State. In view of the critical need to comply with s 174(3) it is prudent to send facsimile copies of communications to the Planning Inspectorate as well as use of the postal system.

Once an appeal has been made the effect is twofold:

(a) the enforcement notice is of no effect pending final determination of the appeal, that is, the notice is suspended (s 175(4));

(b) the appellant is deemed to have made an application for planning permission to the Secretary of State in respect of the development to which the notice relates (s 177(5)).

3.4.3 Preparation and submission of the appeal

It should hardly need stating that particular care is needed in enforcement proceedings in view of the financial consequences of losing the appeal. A close read of the booklet *Enforcement Notice Appeals – A Guide to Procedure* and of Form 14069 is therefore necessary before completing and submitting the form. The considerations mentioned at 3.1.3 above in relation to planning application appeals apply equally to enforcement notice appeals. Having selected the grounds of appeal which are considered relevant, you should proceed to draft the facts upon which reliance is being made to support the appeal.

It is essential to keep a clear distinction between the grounds of the appeal and the facts on which each ground is based; on pp 2–3 of the appeal form, the appellant must specify the relevant facts by making specific statements of fact and not merely by repeating the selected grounds of appeal. The example of a completed Form 14069 which appears below should make this clear.

The example postulates enforcement action being taken against an individual who is carrying on business from a static caravan situated in the curtilage of his house, an activity which the LPA not only seek to terminate within two months of the coming into force of the notice but also seek the removal of the caravan from the site.

Having completed the form the following documents should be sent by first class mail with a covering letter listing the enclosures to the Department of the Environment, Transport and the Regions (PLUP 2), Tollgate House, Houlton Street, Bristol BS2 9DJ:

(a) appeal form (with any supplementary pages);

(b) copy of the enforcement notice.

There is no need to submit the relevant planning fee necessitated by the deemed planning application at this stage: this will be calculated by the Department and a notice requiring payment will be issued shortly after the appeal has been lodged.

Example of completed Form 14069: Town and Country Planning Act 1990 (as amended): Enforcement notice appeal to the Secretary of State for the Environment

- Important: Do not delay. Your completed Appeal form must be received (or posted in time to be received) in the Department before the date on which the Council have stated that the Enforcement Notice shall take effect (see s 8 for more details). You are strongly advised to send the completed form well before this date.

- Before you complete this form, please read the explanatory booklet *Enforcement Notice Appeals – A Guide to Procedure*. If you do not have a copy, the Council can provide one.

1. Appellant's details

(Please complete in BLOCK letters)

Full name and address: *RICHARD CHARLES STAMP, 22 OAK TREE ROAD, WORKTOWN, PLANSHIRE*

Postcode *WT7 3ST*

Telephone number: *WORKTOWN 342–7753*

Reference number: —

Name and address of any agent or professional representative to whom letters should be sent: *AN OTHER & CO, SOLICITORS, 14 UNION STREET, WORKTOWN, PLANSHIRE*

Postcode: *WT1 2BG*

Telephone number: *Worktown 342–8487*

Reference number: *ANO/AB/STAMP*

2. Appeal and grounds

(Please use a separate form for each enforcement notice)

I appeal (on the appellant's behalf)★ under s 174 of the Town and Country Planning Act 1990 (as amended) against the enforcement notice dated 1 March 2001 issued by Worktown District Council relating to land at 22 Oak Tree Road, Worktown.

★delete as appropriate

I appeal on the ground(s) in s 174(2) of the 1990 Act indicated by a cross (X) in the appropriate box below:

☐ Ground (a) that, in respect of any breach of planning control which may be constituted by the matters stated in the notice, planning permission ought to be granted or, as the case may be, the condition or limitation concerned ought to be discharged;

☐ Ground (b) that those matters have not occurred;★★

☐ Ground (c) that those matters (if they occurred) do not constitute a breach of planning control;

☐ Ground (d) that, at the date when the notice was issued, no enforcement action could be taken in respect of any breach of planning control which may be constituted by those matters;

☐ Ground (e) that copies of the enforcement notice were not served as required by s 172;

☐ Ground (f) that the steps required by the notice to be taken, or the activities required by the notice to cease, exceed what is necessary to remedy any breach of planning control which may be constituted by those matters or, as the case may be, to remedy any injury to amenity which has been caused by any such breach;

☐ Ground (g) that any period specified in the notice in accordance with s 173(9) falls short of what should reasonably be allowed.

★★Please note that the only purpose of an appeal on Ground (b) is to maintain that the Council's allegation in the enforcement notice has not occurred, as a matter of fact.

3. Appeal site

Full address of the appeal site and, if possible, the National Grid Reference (refer to an Ordnance Survey map for help)

Postcode (if any)

Please state your legal interest in the appeal site:

★owner/occupier/tenant/lessee/licensee/other (please specify)

★delete as appropriate

4. Other appeals

Have you made any other appeals to the Secretary of State involving this or any related land? Yes/No.

If 'Yes', please provide details:

Type of appeal:

Date of appeal:

DoE reference no (if known):

5. Written representations

Do you agree to have your appeal dealt with on the basis of written statements by the parties and an inspection of the site by an officer of the Department? Yes/No.

If 'Yes', can the whole site be seen clearly from the road or other public land? Yes/No.

(Please indicate by a cross in the appropriate box to help the Department decide whether the officer will need to enter the site and, therefore, have to be accompanied on the site visit.)

(Although you may agree to the appeal being dealt with by written representations, the Secretary of State may find it essential to hold a Public Local Inquiry.)

6. Statement of facts

Please state here the facts in support of each one of the seven grounds appeal (a) to (g) you have marked with an 'X' in Section 2 of this form.

Ground (a)

The caravan to which the enforcement notice relates was placed in the rear garden of the appellant's dwelling house on 14 April 1994 and has been used since that date as an office and workshop in which the appellant carries on business as a watch maker and repairer. The caravan is of the static variety and has electricity, water and telephone services attached. Its dimensions are 36 feet long, 10 feet wide and 9 feet high. The caravan is situated behind a detached garage at a point close to the boundary of the property. Between the caravan and the boundary is a fence 6 feet in height. The caravan is not visible from the highway. As some conifer trees are presently growing on the adjacent property the caravan is not visible other than from the first floor windows of the neighbouring dwelling house.

No deliveries of watches or parts take place at the appeal premises since the appellant uses a Post Office box number. Similarly, customers' watches are returned to them by post. The use of the premises is therefore of a business nature within Use Class B1. This use generates no additional traffic or parking requirement other than generated by the employment of a part time secretary who attends at the appeal premises on three mornings per week.

Ground (f)

The requirement of the enforcement notice to discontinue the use of the land by removal of the caravan is excessive. The caravan was designed for residential use and is stationed within the curtilage of the dwelling house. It is not an act of development merely to station a caravan in the curtilage of a dwelling house since the use of the land for the stationing of the caravan is authorised by s 55(2)(d) of the Town and Country Planning Act 1990.

Ground (g)

The period for compliance of two months is unreasonably short as the appellant will need to find suitable alternative accommodation for his business. Accordingly, a more realistic period for compliance would be six months.

7. Signature

I attach a copy of the relevant enforcement notice to this form.

I confirm that this appeal form contains an appeal/appeals★ against only one enforcement notice and that I have sent a copy of this form to the Council with any supporting documents.

Signature   Date

★delete as appropriate

8. Checking and sending the appeal

Before you send this appeal to the Department, please check that you have:

- completed the whole form, including the statement of facts (Section 6);

- enclosed a copy of the enforcement notice.

Now send one copy of this appeal by first class post to:

Department of the Environment, Transport and the Regions (PLUP 2), Tollgate House, Houlton Street, Bristol BS2 9DJ.

The appeal must arrive (or be posted in time to arrive in the normal course of post) in the Department not later than the day before the date, stated by the Council, for the enforcement notice to take effect.

If the notice takes effect on a Saturday, this will be the preceding Friday or the preceding Thursday if the Friday is a Public Holiday. If the notice takes effect on a Sunday, Monday or public holiday, this will be the last working day before the holiday or the last day on which post is delivered before the Sunday or Holiday.

If you wish to have proof that your appeal has been received by the Department, you should send it by Post Office 'recorded delivery' for which an extra charge is payable. As this service normally takes longer than standard post, please allow extra time if you use it.

To save time, you may fax this appeal form and the Council's enforcement notice to the Department's office in Bristol on (0117) 9878754. You may also deliver, by hand, to any Department of the Environment office; if you do so, please ensure that the receiving officer gives you or your courier a receipt showing the date and time of delivery.

Although a fee may be payable (as explained in the booklet *Enforcement Notice Appeals – A Guide to Procedure*), no money should be enclosed with this appeal form. You will be notified of the fees payable when your appeal has been accepted.

Please send a second copy of the appeal form, and any supporting documents to the Council who issued the enforcement notice.

4 Time-limits

The town and country planning process is regulated by a large number of provisions which seek to impose time-limits within which certain procedural steps are to be taken or rights exercised. Some of these limits are of key importance to the practitioner and must be carefully observed. Others are of a less critical nature, mostly involving action to be taken by the local planning authority (LPA) but which seek to ensure that adequate time is given to interested parties to enable them to express their views on the planning application. Knowledge of these limits is nevertheless important. In this chapter the relevant time-limits are set out in tabular form for ease of reference. The preliminary table below is included, however, in order to give special emphasis to the key time-limits to which reference is most frequently made. (Note: The '1990 Act' is The Town and Country Planning Act 1990; 'GDPO 1995' is the Town and Country Planning (General Development Procedure) Order 1995 SI 1995/419.)

Preliminary table of key time-limits

Step	Period	Provision
Decision on application for planning permission and notification to applicant	8 weeks (unless longer period agreed in writing)	GDPO 1995, Art 20(2)
Implementation of full planning permission	5 years (unless shorter or longer period substituted by LPA)	1990 Act, s 91
Application for approval of reserved matters following grant of outline planning permission	3 years (unless shorter or longer period substituted by LPA)	1990 Act, s 92

Step	Period	Provision
Appeal to Secretary of State against decision of the LPA, or failure to reach a decision	6 months	GDPO 1995, Art 23 (2)
Appeal to the High Court against decision of the Secretary of State	6 weeks	1990 Act, s 288

4.1 Time-limits relevant to an application for planning permission

A more detailed account of the time-limits relevant to a planning application and decision of the LPA is given in the table below.

Step	Period	Provision
(1) Acknowledgment of receipt by LPA	'as soon as is reasonably practicable'	GDPO 1995, Art 5(2)
(2) LPA defers decision until publicity requirements are completed	21 days from date of completion of publicity requirements	GDPO 1995, Art 20(5)
(3) LPA defers decision if applicant is not sole owner of the land or there is an agricultural tenant	21 days from date of service of notice of the application	GDPO 1995, Art 6(5)
(4) LPA defers decision if the application requires an environmental assessment or involves major development or there are adjoining owners or occupiers (places newspaper and site notices, or gives personal notice)	21 days from date publicity completed	GDPO 1995, Art 8
(5) LPA defers decision if planning permission would affect a conservation area or listed building and places newspaper and site notices	21 days from date publicity completed	Planning (Listed Buildings and Conservation Areas) Act 1990, ss 67(6) and 73(1)

Step	Period	Provision
(6) LPA notifies Secretary of State and defers decision if application involves access to a trunk road or is within 67 metres of middle of any highway the Secretary of State is to construct or improve	28 days from date notification given by LPA	GDPO 1995, Art 15(2)
(7) LPA consults with various statutory consultees as specified and defers decision pending representations	14 days from date notification was given by LPA	GDPO 1995, Art 10(4)
(8) LPA notifies parish or community council (if required by that authority) and defers decision pending representations	14 days from date notification was given by LPA	GDPO 1995, Art 13(4)
(9) Decision on application for planning permission and notification to applicant	8 weeks (unless longer period agreed in writing)	GDPO 1995, Art 20(2)
(10) Application for judicial review of LPA's decision	3 months from date of decision	RSC Ord 53, r 4; CPR Pt 50
(11) Appeal to Secretary of State against decision of the LPA, or failure to reach a decision	6 months	GDPO 1995, Art 23(2)
(12) Decision by Secretary of State on appeal from LPA	none[1]	
(13) Appeal to the High Court against the decision of the Secretary of State	6 weeks[2]	1990 Act, s 288(3)
(14) Implementation of full planning permission	5 years (unless shorter or longer period substituted by LPA)	1990 Act, s 91
(15) Application for reserved matters following grant of outline planning permission	3 years (unless shorter or longer period substituted by LPA)	1990 Act, s 92(2)(a)

Step	Period	Provision
(16) Implementation of planning permission following approval of reserved matters	2 years from final approval or 5 years from grant of outline, whichever is the later (unless different periods substituted by LPA)	1990 Act, s 92(2)(b)
(17) Issue of enforcement notice if operational development takes place without planning permission	4 years from date unauthorised operations were substantially completed	1990 Act, s 171B(1)
(18) Issue of enforcement notice if unauthorised material change of use takes place, or there is a failure to comply with a condition or limitation subject to which planning permission has been granted[3]	10 years from the date the breach commenced	1990 Act, s 171B(3)
(19) Complaint to Commissioner for Local Administration	12 months from date of decision	Local Government Act 1974, s 26(4)

Notes

1   While there is no time-limit for the Secretary of State's decision, an appeal which is conducted by submission of written representations is subject to a timetable contained in the Town and Country Planning (Appeals) (Written Representations Procedure) (England) Regulations 2000 SI 2000/1628 (see further, below).

2   Time runs from the date stamp on the decision letter, not from receipt by the appellant (*Griffiths v Secretary of State for the Environment* [1983] 2 AC 51).

3   The 'four-year rule' applies to a breach of planning control consisting of an unauthorised material change of use of a building to use as a single dwelling house.

In *Van Dyck v Secretary of State for the Environment* (1993) JPL 564, it was held that this includes division of a dwelling house into two or more flats or maisonettes.

4.2 Time-limits relevant to an appeal against refusal of planning permission or grant subject to conditions

It will have been noted from the above that six months is available within which to appeal to the Secretary of State. If this right is exercised the time-limits which apply thereafter depend on whether the appeal is to be decided following a hearing, a public local inquiry or, as is the more usual case, after submission of written representations to the Secretary of State. As the latter method is used in most cases, it will be considered first.

4.2.1 Submission of written representations

The timetable is as prescribed by the Town and Country Planning (Appeals) (Written Representations Procedure) (England) Regulations 2000 SI 2000/1628. It can, however, be varied by the Secretary of State in any particular case. The programme is linked to the 'starting date' which is the date on which the Secretary of State gives written notice to the appellant and the local planning authority that he has received all the documents required to enable him to entertain the appeal, or issue of a notice under reg 4 advising the parties of: (a) the starting date; (b) the reference number allocated to the appeal; and (c) the address to which written communications to the Secretary of State about the appeal are to be sent.

The procedure contained in the Town and Country Planning (Appeals) (Written Representations Procedure) (England) Regulations 2000 anticipates that the appellant's case will be contained within the appeal documentation. If, however, further representations are to be made, two copies must be submitted within six weeks of the starting date (reg 7(1) and (4)). Similar arrangements are made in respect of the LPA's case: thus, the LPA's case may (at the election of the LPA) be contained in response to an appeals questionnaire and any documents which the LPA submit with the questionnaire. It will normally be the case, however, that the LPA will wish to make a more detailed submission: reg 7(2) therefore provides that the LPA must submit two copies of their written representations within six weeks of the starting date. The intention, therefore, is that both parties will have completed their submissions by the end of the six week period.

The Secretary of State will 'as soon as practicable' after receipt from one party serve a copy of the relevant written representations on the other party. Both parties may comment on each other's representations within an overall period of nine weeks of the starting date. Documents relevant to the appeal which are submitted out of time may not be considered (reg 7(8)): in *Geha v Secretary of State for the Environment* (1993) 68 P & CR 139, it was held that this provision confers a discretionary power on the Secretary of State to consider documents which are submitted later than in accordance with the prescribed timetable.

The exercise of this discretion is explained in Department of the Environment, Transport and the Regions (DETR) Circular 05/2000, para 14 of which advises that late representations will be considered only in 'extraordinary circumstances'. Examples of circumstances which may be considered to be extraordinary could include a delay induced by a postal strike, ill health of the appellant, or where there has been a last minute change of circumstances of which the inspector ought to know. Clearly it is intended that the parties should adhere to the timetable.

Step		Period	Provision
(1)	Acknowledgment of receipt (the 'starting date') by Secretary of State	'as soon as practicable'	reg 4
(2)	LPA notifies all parties previously notified or consulted about the application or who made representations	2 weeks from receipt of notification of appeal from the Secretary of State	reg 5(1)
(3)	LPA submits questionnaire and appeal documents to Secretary of State	2 weeks after starting date	reg 6(1)
(4)	LPA submits representations to Secretary of State	6 weeks after starting date	reg 7(3)
(5)	Representations submitted by all other parties to Secretary of State	6 weeks after starting date	reg 5(2)
(6)	Appellant and the LPA may make further representations in reply to submissions of the other party	9 weeks after starting date	reg 7(7)
(7)	Appellant and LPA comment on any representations received from other parties	14 days from sending of copies by Secretary of State	reg 8(2)
(8)	Decision of Secretary of State	none	—

4.2.2 Hearing

Provision in respect of hearings is made by the Town and Country
Planning (Hearings Procedure) (England) Rules 2000 SI 2000/1626.
For discussion of these rules see 3.1.6. The relevant timetable is as
follows.

Step	Period	Provision
(1) Secretary of State receives appeal, confirms validity, notifies the parties of the 'starting date'	none specified	—
(2) LPA supplies Secretary of State with details of statutory parties	forthwith, after receiving notice of appeal	r 4(1)
(3) LPA notifies all parties previously notified or consulted about the application or who made representations	2 weeks after starting date	r 4(2)
(4) LPA submits questionnaire and appeal documents to Secretary of State and appellant	2 weeks after starting date	r 4(2)
(5) LPA and appellant submit hearing statements to Secretary of State	6 weeks after starting date	r 6(1)
(6) Secretary of State may issue request for further information about matters in the hearing statement	such period as Secretary of State may reasonably require	r 6(2)
(7) Third parties submit written comments on the appeal to Secretary of State	6 weeks after starting date	r 6(3)
(8) Secretary of State sends copy of each party's hearing statement to the other party	as soon as practicable	r 6(5)
(9) Appellant and LPA submit comments on the other party's hearing statement and of any comments made by a third parties	9 weeks after starting date	r 6(4)
(10) Secretary of State notifies parties of date time and place of hearing	at least 4 weeks prior to hearing unless a shorter period is agreed with the appellant and the LPA	r 7(2)

Step	Period	Provision
(11) Hearing commences	not later than 12 weeks after the starting date or earliest practicable date thereafter	r 7(1)

4.2.3 Public local inquiry

Public local inquiries are regulated by the Town and Country Planning (Inquiries Procedure) (England) Rules 2000 SI 2000/1624 or by the Town and Country Planning (Determination by Inspectors) (Inquiries Procedure) (England) Rules 2000 SI 2000/1625. Most appeals are transferred to the inspector for decision and hence the latter rules will apply. Similar timetables are contained in each of the procedural rules and hence only that contained in SI 2000/1625 is set out below. Both commence by reference to the 'relevant date', that is, the date on which the Secretary of State notifies the parties that an inquiry is to take place. Both sets of Rules encompass not only planning appeals but also listed building consent and conservation area consent appeals.

Both sets of Rules make provision for the possibility of a pre-inquiry meeting between the inspector and the parties for the purposes of identifying the main issues. The Secretary of State has advised, however, in DETR Circular 05/2000 that this aspect of the procedure is unlikely to be invoked except in cases of major importance. Moreover, r 7(2) of the Determination by Inspectors Rules provides that a pre-inquiry meeting should be held where the inspector considers that inquiry is likely to last for eight days or more, but otherwise is only to hold a pre-inquiry meeting if he considers it necessary.

In the likely absence of a pre-inquiry meeting the timetable is such that the inquiry will be scheduled to take place within 20 weeks of the Secretary of State's initial notification to the parties that an inquiry will be held (or 22 weeks if the Secretary of State rather than the inspector is to decide the appeal). This initial date is the 'starting date'.

Step	Period	Provision
(1) Secretary of State receives appeal, confirms validity, notifies the parties of the 'starting date'	none specified	—
(2) LPA supplies Secretary of State with details of statutory parties	forthwith, after receiving notice of appeal	r 4(1)
(3) LPA notifies all parties previously notified or consulted about the application or who made representations	2 weeks after starting date	r 4(4)
(4) LPA submits questionnaire and appeal documents to Secretary of State and appellant	2 weeks after starting date	r 4(4)
(5) LPA and appellant submit their statements of case to Secretary of State	6 weeks after starting date	r 6(1) and (3)
(6) Secretary of State may issue request for further information about matters in the statement of case	such period as the Secretary of State may specify	r 6(8)
(7) LPA and appellant may submit written comments on the other party's statement of case to the Secretary of State	9 weeks after starting date	r 6(14)
(8) Secretary of State sends copy of each party's comments on the other party's statement of case to the other party	as soon as practicable	r 6(14)
(9) Secretary of State notifies parties of date time and place of inquiry	at least 4 weeks prior to inquiry unless a shorter period is agreed with the appellant and the LPA	r 10(2)
(10) LPA and appellant submit proofs of evidence and summaries to Secretary of State	at least 4 weeks prior to inquiry	r 14(4)
(11) LPA and appellant submit statement of common ground to Secretary of State	at least 4 weeks prior to inquiry	r 15(1)

Step	Period	Provision
(12) Inquiry commences	not later than 20 weeks after the starting date or earliest practicable date thereafter	r 10(1)

4.3   Time-limits relevant to issue of an enforcement notice

In enforcement proceedings the timetable is calculated from the date of issue of the enforcement notice. This document is to be retained by the LPA and copies of it served on the owner and on the occupier and on any other person having an interest in the land. This is made clear by s 172(2) of the 1990 Act.

Step	Period	Provision
(1) Issue of enforcement notice	4 years from date unauthorised operations were substantially completed, or 10 years from commencement of a material change of use[1]	1990 Act, s 171B(1)(3)
(2) Entry in register of enforcement and stop notices	14 days from issue	GDPO 1995, Art 26(6)
(3) Service of copies	28 days from issue	1990 Act, s 172(3)
(4) Notice comes into effect	as specified in notice but not less than 28 days from completion of service	1990 Act, s 172(3)
(5) Appeal to Secretary of State	before date specified in the notice on which it is to come into effect[2]	1990 Act, s 174(3)
(6) Time for compliance	as specified in notice[3]	1990 Act, s 173(9)

Notes

1   The four-year limitation period applies to an unauthorised material change of use consisting of the change of use of a building to use as a single dwelling house.

2 Notice of appeal may be effected by letter posted so that in the ordinary course of post it would be delivered to the Secretary of State before the date specified in the notice.

3 The enforcement notice is suspended by an appeal to the Secretary of State (s 175(4) of the 1990 Act). The period for compliance is relevant once again if the appeal is dismissed.

4.4 Time-limits relevant to an appeal against issue of an enforcement notice

The critical time-limit in enforcement appeals is that relevant to the submission of the appeal to the Secretary of State. This must be achieved before the end of the first period stated in the notice, that is, before the date specified in the notice as the date on which it is to come into effect. All that is required to preserve the appellant's right of appeal is submission of a notice of appeal: details of the grounds of appeal and facts can be submitted later following a written request from the Secretary of State. In the table which appears below, it is assumed that a bare notice of appeal is given in the first instance.

4.4.1 Enforcement – public local inquiry

Public local inquiries are regulated by the Town and Country Planning (Enforcement) (Inquiries Procedure) Rules 1992 SI 1992/1903. Pre-inquiry procedure is regulated by the Town and Country Planning (Enforcement Notices and Appeals) Regulations 1991 SI 1991/2804. In the table which appears below, references to a 'reg' are to SI 1991/2804 and references to a 'rule' are to SI 1992/1903.

Step	Period	Provision
(1) Appellant lodges notice of appeal	before date specified in the notice on which it is to come into effect	1990 Act, s 174(3)
(2) Secretary of State acknowledges receipt of appeal and notifies that an inquiry is to take place. The date of notification is the 'relevant date'	none specified	—

Step	Period	Provision
(3) Secretary of State requests grounds of appeal and brief statement of facts	none specified	—
(4) Appellant lodges grounds of appeal and brief statement of facts	14 days from date of Secretary of State's request	reg 5
(5) Secretary of State gives notice of date, time and place of inquiry	none specified, but inquiry to be held not later than 24 weeks after the relevant date	r 11(1)
(6) LPA serves statement of case on Secretary of State, appellant and any other person on whom copy of the notice was served. LPA must also state the submissions to be put forward including (a) a summary of the LPA's response to each ground of appeal and (b) if the LPA would be willing to grant planning permission, the conditions they would wish to impose	if inquiry is to be held less than 18 weeks after the relevant date, then at least 6 weeks before inquiry; in all other cases, not later than 12 weeks after relevant date	r 8(1) and reg 7(2)
(7) Appellant serves statement of case on Secretary of State, LPA and any other person on whom a copy of the enforcement notice was served	if inquiry is to be held less than 18 weeks after the relevant date then at least 3 weeks before inquiry; in all other cases not later than 15 weeks after the relevant date	r 8(2)
(8) Appellant may make written request to Secretary of State for representative of a government department to appear at the inquiry if LPA propose to rely on their view on the appeal	not less than 2 weeks before inquiry	r 13(1)

Step	Period	Provision
(9) Written statements (proofs) of evidence and summaries submitted to Secretary of State and LPA	at least 3 weeks before inquiry	r 14(3)
(10) Inspector notifies appellant and LPA if he decides to take into account new evidence or new matter of fact after close of inquiry	3 weeks allowed for representations or request for re-opening inquiry	r 18(3)
(11) Notification of decision	none specified	—

4.4.2 Enforcement – submission of written representations

Unlike s 78 appeals against refusal of planning permission, enforcement written representations appeals are not yet the subject of a procedural code embodied in a statutory instrument. The provisions of the Town and Country Planning (Enforcement Notices and Appeals) Regulations 1991 do, however, apply in the initial stages of the appeal, so that the LPA are required to serve on the Secretary of State and the appellant: (a) a statement which summarises the LPA's response to each ground of appeal pleaded by the appellant; and (b) a statement whether the authority would be prepared to grant planning permission for the matters alleged to be in breach of planning control and, if so, the conditions they would wish to impose. These submissions must be made not later than 28 days from the date of a notice from the Secretary of State to the LPA (reg 7(2)).

5 Planning Fees

A system of fees payable in respect of various types of application under the town and country planning legislation was introduced by s 87 of the Local Government, Planning and Land Act 1980. The details of the fees which are to be paid and the legal structure of the fees regime are contained in the Town and Country Planning (Fees for Applications and Deemed Applications) Regulations 1989 SI 1989/193, as amended by SIs 1990/2473, 1991/2735, 1992/1817, 1992/3052, 1993/317 and 1997/37. Following the consolidation of the town and country planning legislation in 1990, instruments regulating planning fees are now made under s 303 of the Town and Country Planning Act 1990 (the '1990 Act'). The most recent of these instruments contains the current scale of fees. In this chapter references to 'the Regulations' mean the 1989 Regulations, as amended.

Practitioners should note that there are many occasions on which an exemption applies from the normal requirement to pay a planning fee and that there are some concessions which permit the payment of a smaller fee than would otherwise be payable. Also, not every type of application under the 1990 Act attracts a fee. These three categories are explained further, below. Practitioners are, however, recommended to consult Department of the Environment (DoE) Circular 31/92 which contains useful practical advice about the fees system.

5.1 Applications under the 1990 Act

5.1.1 Instances where a fee is payable

Under regs 1(2), 10A and 11A, a fee is *prima facie* payable in respect of any of the following applications:

(a) application for planning permission, whether full or outline (includes a 'retrospective' application);

(b) application for approval of reserved matters;

(c) application for consent for the display of an advertisement;

(d) deemed application for planning permission on making an appeal against an enforcement notice;

(e) application for certificate of lawfulness of existing use or development;

(f) application for certificate of lawfulness of proposed use or development;

(g) application to the local planning authority (LPA) for determination whether their prior approval will be required in relation to development specified in Pts 6, 7, 24 and 31 of Sched 2 to the Town and Country Planning (General Permitted Development) Order 1995 SI 1995/418 ('GPDO 1995').

5.1.2 Instances where no fee is payable

The 1989 Regulations do not contain a list of applications for which no fee is payable, but as they are not expressly included the following may be taken to be excluded:

(a) application for listed building consent;

(b) application for conservation area consent;

(c) application to top, lop, etc, a tree subject to a tree preservation order;

(d) application for scheduled monument consent;

(e) appeal to the Secretary of State against refusal of planning permission by the LPA or grant subject to conditions;

(f) appeal to the Secretary of State against refusal of a certificate of lawfulness of existing use or development;

(g) appeal to the Secretary of State against refusal of a certificate of lawfulness of proposed use or development.

5.2 The scale of fees

The fees payable with an application are specified in Sched 1 to the 1989 Regulations. The following table contains the current prescribed fee scale which came into force on 1 October 1997. At first sight, the prescribed scale is not a model of clarity, but the observations below will assist the reader in locating the relevant fee.

Table 1: Planning fees

Proposed operational developments

---

(1) The erection of dwelling houses (other than development within category 6 below).

Fee payable:

(a) Where the application is for outline planning permission, £190 for each 0.1 hectare of the site area, subject to a maximum of £4,750.

(b) In other cases, £190 for each dwelling house to be created by the development, subject to a maximum of £9,500.

---

(2) The erection of buildings (other than buildings within categories 1, 3, 4, 5 or 7).

Fee payable:

(a) Where the application is for outline planning permission, £190 for each 0.1 hectare of the site area, subject to a maximum of £4,750.

(b) In other cases:

(i) where no floor space is to be created by the development, £95;

(ii) where the area of gross floor space to be created by the development does not exceed 40 sq metres, £95;

(iii) where the area of gross floor space to be created by the development exceeds 40 sq metres but does not exceed 75 sq metres, £190; and

(iv) where the area of gross floor space to be created by the development exceeds 75 sq metres, £190 for each 75 sq metres subject to a maximum of £9,500.

---

(3) The erection, on land used for the purposes of agriculture, of buildings to be used for agricultural purposes (other than buildings coming within category 4).

Fee payable:

(a) Where the application is for outline planning permission, £190 for each 0.1 hectare of the site area, subject to a maximum of £4,750.

(b) In other cases:

(i) where the area of gross floor space to be created by the development does not exceed 465 sq metres, £35;

(ii) where the area of gross floor space to be created by the development exceeds 465 sq metres but does not exceed 540 sq metres, £190;

(iii) where the area of gross floor space to be created by the development exceeds 540 sq metres, £190 for the first 540 sq metres and £190 for each 75 sq metres in excess of the figure subject to a maximum of £9,500.

---

(4) The erection of glasshouses on land used for the purposes of agriculture.

Fee payable:

(a) Where the area of gross floor space to be created by the development does not exceed 465 sq metres, £35.

(b) Where the area of gross floor space to be created by the development exceeds 465 sq metres, £1,085.

(5) The erection, alteration or replacement of plant or machinery.

Fee payable:

£190 for each 0.1 hectare of the site area, subject to a maximum of £9,500.

(6) The enlargement, improvement or other alteration of existing dwelling houses.

Fee payable:

(a) Where the application relate to one dwelling house, £95.

(b) Where the application relates to 2 or more dwelling houses, £190.

(7) (a) The carrying-out of operations (including the erection of a building) within the curtilage of an existing dwelling house, for purposes ancillary to the enjoyment of the dwelling house as such, or the erection or construction of gates, fences, walls or other means of enclosure along a boundary of the curtilage of an existing dwelling house; or

(b) the construction of car parks, service roads and other means of access on land used for the purposes of a single undertaking, where the development is required for purpose incidental to the existing use of the land.

Fee payable:

£95.

(8) The carrying-out of any operations connected with exploratory drilling for oil or natural gas.

Fee payable:

£190 for each 0.1 hectare of the site area, subject to a maximum of £14,250.

(9) The carrying-out of any operations not coming within any of the above categories.

Fee payable:

£95 for each 0.1 hectare of the site area, subject to a maximum of:

(a) in the case of operations for the winning and working of minerals, £14,250;

(b) in other cases, £950.

Proposed development comprising a material change of use

(10) The change of use of a building to use as one or more separate dwelling houses.

Fee payable:

(a) Where the change is from a previous use as a single dwelling house to use as two or more single dwelling houses, £190 for each additional dwelling house to be created by the development, subject to a maximum of £9,500.

(b) in other cases, £190 for each dwelling house to be created by the development, subject to a maximum of £9,500.

(11) (a) The use of land for the disposal of refuse or waste materials or for the deposit of material remaining after minerals have been extracted from land; or

(b) the use of land for the storage of minerals in the open.

Fee payable:

£95 for each 0.1 hectare of the site area, subject to a maximum of £14,250.

(12) The making of a material change in the use of a building or land (other than a material change of use coming within any of the above categories).

Fee payable: £190.

Table 2: Fees in respect of applications for consent to display advertisements

(1) Advertisements displayed on business premises, on the forecourt of business premises or on other land within the curtilage of business premises, wholly with reference to all or any of the following matters:

(a) the nature of the business or other activity carried out on the premises;

(b) the goods sold or the services provided on the premises; or

(c) the name and qualifications of the person carrying on such business or activity or supplying such goods or services.

Fee payable: £50.

(2) Advertisements for the purpose of directing members of the public to, or otherwise drawing attention to the existence of, business premises which are in the same locality as the site on which the advertisement is to be displayed but which are not visible from that site.

Fee payable: £50.

(3) All other advertisements.

Fee payable: £190.

The following observations will help locate in Table 1 the most commonly applicable fees:

(a) alterations to a dwelling house – £95 (see 6(a) above);

(b) erection of a dwelling house – £190 (see 1(b) above);

(c) conversion to flats of a dwelling house – £190 for each additional unit of accommodation (see 10(a) above);

(d) material change of use – £190 (see 12 above);

(e) new shop front – £95 (see 2(b)(i) above);

(f) construction of an access to a highway – £95 (see 7(b) above).

5.3   Dealing with outline applications

Examination of the fees scale shows that applications for outline planning permission are charged in accordance with the area of land involved, a multiple of £190 being charged for each 0.1 of a hectare involved up to a maximum of £4,750. This applies to, for example:

(a) housing developments (see 1(a) above);

(b) commercial developments (see 2(a) above);

(c) agricultural buildings (see 3(a) above). This is to be contrasted with applications for full planning permission.

Full applications are charged in accordance with the number of dwellings (housing development), or the gross floor space to be created by the proposal (commercial developments and agricultural buildings), see 1(b), 2(b) and 3(b) above. For outline applications fees will need to be paid in at least two stages; first, in respect of the outline proposal and secondly, in respect of the subsequent application for approval of the reserved matters. The first stage involves a simple calculation of the site area. The maximum fee of £4,750 will be payable if the site exceeds 2.5 hectares, since £190 x 25 x 0.1 = £4,750. Expressed in terms of acres, as one hectare = 2.471 acres the maximum fee is reached with a site of 2.471 x 2.5 = 6.18 acres. The second fee will be that payable as if the application had been for full planning permission in the first place, that is, based on the number of dwellings or the gross floor space, as appropriate, with a maximum fee of £9,500. It must be borne in mind, however, that not all applications for approval of the reserved matters will be made at the same time, or even in respect of all of the development for which outline planning permission has been granted. If approval is sought in stages, a full fee is payable every time an application for approval of a reserved matter is made, but only until the total amount paid by the applicant is equal to the fee that would have been paid had approval been sought for all the reserved matters together. When this stage is reached any subsequent application is charged at £190. Some examples should make this clear.

Example 1

A developer proposes to construct 40 houses on a site of 3 hectares. If the developer applies for full planning permission the fee would be £190 x 40 dwellings = £7,600. If the developer applied for outline planning permission the fee would be £190 per 0.1 hectare, that is, £190 x 30 = £5,700. But, since the maximum fee for an outline application is £4,750, only £4,750 is payable. Having obtained outline planning permission, the developer seeks approval of all reserved matters in one application. The fee is £190 x 40 dwellings = £7,600.

Example 2

A developer proposes to construct 30 houses, 10 flats and 10 maisonettes on a site of 2 hectares. If the developer applied for full planning permission the fee would be £190 x 50 dwellings = £9,500. If the developer applied for outline planning permission the fee would be £190 x 0.1 hectare, that is, £190 x 20 = £3,800. Having obtained outline planning permission the developer seeks approval of some reserved matters in respect of the 30 houses. The fee is £190 x 30 dwellings = £5,700. He then seeks approval of the same reserved matters in respect of the flats and maisonettes. The fee is £190 x 20 dwellings = £3,800. The developer has therefore now paid (in respect of reserved matters applications) a total of £9,500 (£5,700 + £3,800). Thus, all further applications for approval of remaining reserved matters are charged at the flat rate fee of £190.

5.3.1 Other applications requiring payment of a planning fee

An application for a certificate of lawfulness of existing use or development, or for a certificate of lawfulness of proposed use or development under ss 191 and 192, respectively, of the 1990 Act are both subject to a fee scheme contained in reg 10A of the Regulations. The fee in respect of a s 191 application is the same as would be payable in respect of a planning application for the same development as that specified in the application, except where a certificate is sought in respect of a failure to comply with any condition or limitation, subject to which planning permission has previously been granted. In this instance a fee of £95 is payable.

In the case of a s 192 application the relevant fee is one-half of the fee that would be payable for a planning application for the same proposal.

5.4 Time for payment and disputed fees

5.4.1 Payment of the fee

The relevant fee must be paid at the time when the application is made and the amount of the fee must be sent to the local planning authority, normally the district council (or, were appropriate the unitary authority), together with the application (reg 3(3) of the Regulations). It should be noted that where an application is not accompanied by a fee, or where the incorrect fee is included, the application is not void but the eight-week period within which the local planning authority must reach its decision to comply with Art 20(2)(a) of the Town and Country Planning (General Development Procedure) Order 1995 SI 1995/419 does not run until the correct fee is received by the local planning authority (Art 20(3)(c)). As you will wish to progress the application as quickly as possible, it is a useful precaution (except in straightforward cases) to contact the LPA and ask their opinion on the correct fee payable. An example would be the calculation of the fee payable where the application involves an element of operational development, for example, an extension to a building, but the main purpose of the application is to change the use of the property. Such an application is charged at £190, but the practitioner might reasonably think that £380 was payable and be unsure whether payment of a fee of £190 would leave the application incomplete and hence temporarily unconsidered. Even where a potential overpayment is identified, it is desirable to clarify the matter with the local planning authority as it may take some time to recover an overpayment.

There is no provision for refund of fees which have been correctly tendered, where the application is withdrawn. A refund can, however, be made in respect of an application which is found to be invalid or where the fee paid is unneccesary.

The amount of the fee payable is always determined on the basis of the application as submitted to the local planning authority. Thus, if an amendment is made by agreement to an existing application, or if the local planning authority require submission of details of one or more reserved matters before determining an outline application, there is no provision for an additional charge.

5.4.2 Disputed fees

There is no formal procedure available to resolve fee disputes although LPAs are urged by DoE Circular 31/92, para 28, to avoid delaying applications and therefore to resolve disputes quickly. Where agreement cannot be reached, the applicant may exercise the right of appeal to the Secretary of State arising from the failure of the LPA to determine the application (s 78(2) of the 1990 Act). If the Secretary of State regards the fee paid as inadequate he will have no jurisdiction to decide the appeal in which case the applicant must pay the required fee, as determined by the Secretary of State, to the LPA who will then determine the application.

5.5 Exemptions

Regulations 4–9 of the 1989 Regulations provide for 11 circumstances in which no fee is payable. These are summarised as follows:

(a) Regulation 4 – Applications for alteration, extension or operations in the curtilage of a dwelling house to provide access or facilities for a resident (or prospective resident) disabled person. Applications relating to other premises are also exempt if the purpose of the development is to provide access for disabled members of the public.

(b) Regulation 5 – If permitted development rights have been removed by a direction made under Art 4 of the GPDO 1995, no fee is payable for an application necessitated by the direction. A similar exemption applies if GPDO 1995 rights are removed by a condition attached to a grant of planning permission.

(c) Regulation 6 – If change of use rights under the Use Classes Order of 1987 have been removed by a condition attached to a grant of planning permission, no fee is required in respect of a proposed change of use to one in the same class as the existing use.

(d) Regulation 7 – If planning permission has been granted, a further application by the same applicant for a modified proposal is exempt if made within 12 months of the grant. Only one further application qualifies under this provision.

(e) Regulation 8 – Six exemptions are specified by this provision:

- the application is made following withdrawal of a previous application before decision;
- an application is made following a refusal of planning permission by the local authority or the Secretary of State on appeal to him or following a call-in of the application;
- an application is made following an appeal to the Secretary of State under s 78(2) of the 1990 Act (appeal in default of a decision);
- an application for approval of one or more reserved matters is made following the withdrawal of an application for the same reserved matters before a decision was made on it;
- an application for approval of one or more reserved matters is made following a refusal to approve such matters;
- an application for approval of one or more reserved matters is made following an appeal to the Secretary of State under s 78(2) of the 1990 Act.

All of these six exemptions are subject to the same qualifications that is, that the exempt application is made in relation to proposed development of the same character or description within 12 months of the previous decision or withdrawal, and by the same applicant. Only one further application qualifies under this provision.

(f) Regulation 9 – Application to consolidate two or more existing grants of planning permission for winning and working of minerals, provided no further development proposal is included in the application.

5.6 Concessionary fees

Part I of Sched 1 to the 1989 Regulations specifies the following concessions from the application of the normal fee scale. These do not, however, constitute exemptions:

(a) all applications by or on behalf of parish or community councils are charged at 50 % of the fee which would be payable by a private developer;

(b) an application by or on behalf of non–profit-making club, society or other organisation whose objects are the provision of facilities for sport or recreation if relating to playing fields for their own use is charged at £190;

(c) an application (under s 73 of the 1990 Act) to modify or discharge a condition subject to which planning permission has previously been granted is charged at £95. This encompasses so called 'renewal' applications where a grant is sought to enable a development to continue at the end of a specified period imposed by a condition, or where a grant of planning permission has previously been obtained but has not yet been implemented. It does not, however, include the case where a time limit has already expired;

(d) an application for planning permission under s 73A of the 1990 Act in respect of development already carried out without complying with a condition or limitation attached to a previous grant of planning permission is subject to a fee of £95.

Where the developer submits more than one application for planning permission on the same date relating to the same site but for different forms of development, the relevant fee for each proposal must be calculated separately; the fee which is payable is the highest of the individual fees plus one-half of the total fees which would normally be payable in respect of the other applications.

Note: This concession does not apply where the developer submits two identical applications with the object of making an appeal to the Secretary of State in respect of one application in the event that planning permission is refused or granted subject to unacceptable conditions. In these circumstances, the developer must pay the full fee for both applications.

6 Recovery of Costs

The largest single activity of a local planning authority (LPA) is the process of dealing with planning applications. While the majority of planning applications are successful, there will inevitably be difficulties with applications which are the subject of objections or in respect of which there are policy or other reasons which indicate that planning permission is unlikely to be forthcoming. This is particularly so where it is clear that the provisions of the development plan show that a favourable decision is unlikely. Applicants for planning permission will often wish to go to great lengths to persuade the LPA that planning permission should be granted especially in instances where the development plan does not contain provisions which are directly applicable to the application site. This may involve pre-application discussions with planning officers, preparing written rebuttals of reasons for recommended refusal, addressing the planning committee, as well as submitting and progressing the planning application. If, in the end, a successful conclusion is reached can all or any of the expenses which are thereby incurred be recovered? To this question there is a simple answer? 'No.' No expenses in progressing a planning application are ever recoverable from the LPA, not even the planning fee. A moment's thought will show that this is justifiable for if it were otherwise, LPAs would have an incentive to decline to grant planning permission and this would therefore fetter the discretion of the LPA under s 70 of the Town and Country Planning Act 1990 (the '1990 Act').

The principle that costs incurred by applicants are non-recoverable applies also to other types of application made under the 1990 Act 1990, for example, for a certificate of lawfulness of proposed use or development or a certificate of lawfulness of existing use or development. By the same token, however, the administrative costs incurred by the LPA in dealing with an application which is doomed to failure are non-recoverable even if these costs exceed the planning fee which may be payable.

Where, however, it is thought appropriate to make an appeal to the Secretary of State against a decision of the LPA, the general principle is that each party to the appeal is responsible for their own costs. To this general principle there is an important exception as the Secretary of State is empowered to award costs, though this is subject to a self-imposed restriction to those cases where he considers that a party to the appeal has behaved 'unreasonably'. The scope of the power to award costs and the definition of unreasonable behaviour will now be examined.

6.1   Power of Secretary of State to award costs

This power is derived from ss 320, 322 and 322A of the 1990 Act and s 250(5) of the Local Government Act 1972. The effect of the legislation is that the Secretary of State can award costs in planning appeals, enforcement appeals and any other matter in respect of which the Secretary of State is empowered to convene a public local inquiry. The power is not limited, however, to appeals decided by the Secretary of State following a public local inquiry as it also applies to:

(a) appeals decided by the Secretary of State following a hearing before a person appointed by him (an inspector);

(b) appeals decided by inspectors following a public local inquiry or a hearing before an inspector;

(c) appeals in which the public local inquiry or hearing does not take place.

The Secretary of State also has the power to make awards of costs in respect of some appeals determined by written representations, particularly enforcement appeals. Written representations appeals in respect of refusal of planning permission or grant subject to conditions are currently not included. The same scheme will eventually apply as in all such cases; thus, the usual criterion of 'unreasonable behaviour' must be satisfied before an award can be made. This concept is explained in Department of the Environment Circular 8/93 entitled *Awards of Costs Incurred in Planning and Other (Including Compulsory Purchase Order) Proceedings*, which points out that the word 'unreasonable' is to be given its ordinary meaning in accordance with the decision of the High Court in *Manchester CC v Secretary of State for the Environment and Mercury Communications Ltd* (1988) JPL 774. It should be noted, however, that less than one-third of applications for costs do not succeed.

6.2   Unreasonable behaviour

The mere fact that an appeal to the Secretary of State has been successful is not sufficient to justify a claim that the LPA has behaved unreasonably. Circular 8/93 advises that it will be necessary to show that unreasonable behaviour has caused the applicant for costs to incur or waste expenses unnecessarily either:

(a) because it should not have been necessary for the case to come before the Secretary of State for determination; or

(b) because of the manner in which another party has behaved in the proceedings (for example, because an arranged inquiry or hearing had to be cancelled or extended, resulting in wasted preparatory work or unnecessary additional expense).

Many examples of unreasonable behaviour which may cause the Secretary of State to exercise his discretionary power to award costs are given in the Circular and in reported planning appeal decisions. Some of the more significant examples contained in the Circular are summarised below.

Unreasonable refusal of planning permission

(a) The LPA are expected to produce evidence to substantiate each reason for refusal by reference to the development plan and all other material considerations. If they cannot do so, costs may be awarded against them. Each reason for refusal will be examined for evidence that the provisions of the development plan, relevant departmental guidance and judicial authority were properly taken into account.

(b) Refusal of an application which accords with material policies or proposals in the development plan and the LPA are unable to show that there are any other material considerations supporting such a refusal.

(c) Slavish adherence to a development plan which is out of date unless the LPA can show they are taking all reasonable steps to bring the plan up to date.

(d) Acceptance of local opposition where a grant of planning permission involves no material departure from plans or policies and there are no other planning reasons why permission should be refused.

(e) Refusal based mainly on preference for a different external appearance; LPAs should not seek to control the detailed design of buildings unless the sensitive character of the setting for the development justifies it.

(f) Refusal of a revised application which has been altered consistent with advice contained in a previous unsuccessful appeal decision which indicated that a revised application on specified lines would be acceptable.

(g) Refusal of an application for approval of reserved matters, raising objections more appropriate to the outline application stage, but the LPA are unable to show good reason on appeal for their stance.

(h) Failure to renew a temporary planning permission without good reason, for example, a material change in planning circumstances.

Grant of planning permission subject to conditions

(i) Imposition of a condition which fails to meet the criteria in Circular 1/85 (now replaced by Circular 11/95), that is, that the condition should be necessary, reasonable, enforceable, precise and relevant to planning and to the proposed development.

Unreasonable issue of an enforcement notice

(j) The sole reason for issue of the notice is the lack of planning permission for the development enforced against but there are no significant planning objections to the breach of planning control.

(k) Inadequate statement of reasons for taking enforcement action or lack of reasonable grounds for concluding that a breach of planning control has occurred.

(l) If the LPA feel compelled to withdraw an enforcement notice, effectively conceding that it was not expedient to have issued it, for example, if it is so incorrectly drafted or so technically defective that it could not be corrected or varied by the Secretary of State, so that an appeal and the expense involved were unnecessary.

Conduct of the LPA

(m) In an appeal under s 78(2) of the 1990 Act the LPA failed to give specific and adequate reasons for not reaching a decision within the time-limit.

(n) Refusal to discuss the planning application (or the possibility of grant of planning permission where an enforcement notice has been issued) or refusal to provide information which could reasonably be expected to have been provided, if it is concluded that a more helpful approach would have enabled the appeal to be avoided.

(o) Failure to seek further details from the applicant if planning permission is refused for lack of detail.

(p) Failure to undertake reasonable investigations to establish whether or not there has been a breach of planning control before issuing an enforcement notice; while service of a planning contravention notice is not obligatory, failure to do so can be taken into account.

(q) A new reason for refusal is introduced at a late stage in the proceedings, or dropped, or an enforcement notice is withdrawn.

(r) The proceedings have been unnecessarily prolonged due to the LPA's failure to co-operate in settling agreed facts or supplying relevant information so that the proceedings are adjourned or prolonged unnecessarily.

(s) Failure to comply with procedural requirements which has seriously prejudiced the appellant and caused the inquiry to be adjourned or unnecessarily prolonged causing the appellant extra expense.

Unreasonably making an appeal

(t) The appellant appeals against refusal of planning permission not withstanding an earlier appeal decision from which it is plain that the development should not be authorised.

(u) It is obvious from official statements of planning policy or case law that the appeal has no reasonable prospect of success, for example, a proposed major development in a green belt area.

(v) The decision of the LPA has been made in accordance with the development plan and policy guidance but the appellant fails to produce substantial evidence to support the contention that there are material considerations which would justify an exception to the policies of the development plan.

Conduct of the appellant

(w) Failure to comply with procedural rules, provide an adequate pre-inquiry statement or introducing a new ground of appeal when it is too late to postpone the start of the inquiry.

(x) The appellant is wilfully unco-operative, for example, by refusing to explain the grounds of appeal or refusing to discuss the appeal.

(y) The appellant withdraws his appeal so soon before the inquiry date that there is insufficient time to inform other parties and their witnesses who thereby incur abortive expenditure in attendance costs.

Examples of unreasonable behaviour which are shown by reported planning appeal decisions made by the Secretary of State are:

(a) failure by the LPA to determine the application – (1988) 2 PAD 44;

(b) failure by appellant to prepare their case satisfactorily, resulting in extra and abortive work at the inquiry – (1993) 8 PAD 115;

(c) appellant responsible for an unnecessary adjournment and submission of proofs of evidence of two witnesses who were not called to give evidence – (1992) 7 PAD 167;

(d) LPA unreasonably required appellant to enter into a planning agreement involving a commuted payment for municipal car parking when no action had been taken by the authority to identify a suitable site – (1991) 6 PAD 206;

(e) failure by the LPA to provide accommodation for the second day of an inquiry – (1988) 3 PAD 58;

(f) refusal of planning permission on grounds of objection not relevant to the planing merits – (1987) JPL 811;

(g) failure by the LPA to support grounds of refusal of planning permission by substantial evidence – (1986) JPL 219, 222, 226;

(h) failure by the LPA to grant planning permission contrary to views expressed by the inspector at a previous inquiry – (1984) JPL 744;

(i) enforcement notice served without reasonable prior investigations – (1984) JPL 755;

(j) failure of appellant to attend inquiry – (1984) JPL 761;

(k) making an appeal where no significant change in planning circumstances had occurred since a previous unsuccessful appeal – (1984) JPL 765;

(l) refusal of planning permission by the LPA on grounds of prematurity without identifying any real harm to the development plan process – (1995) PAD 1;

(m) imposition of an unreasonable condition on a grant of planning permission – (1995) PAD 575;

(n) failure by the LPA to provide an appeal statement following an appeal against an enforcement notice, leading to the enforcement notice being quashed – (2000) JPL 762.

Practitioners should note that many more examples of decisions under earlier Circulars 73/65, 69/71 and 2/87 are listed in Purdue and Fraser, *Planning Decisions Digest* (see Chapter 10). It must be emphasised, however, that an award of costs is discretionary and will not necessarily be made simply because the party seeking costs can establish one of the cited examples. The Secretary of State's decision is, nevertheless, capable of judicial review (*R v Secretary of State for the Environment ex p Wild* (1985) JPL 753). It was also held in *Botton v Secretary of State for the Environment* (1992) JPL 236 that an appeal to the High Court is competent under s 288 of the 1990 Act. It may be noted, however, that as the appellant in that case had also applied for judicial review it was not necessary for Roch J to decide which procedure was correct.

6.3 Procedure for claiming costs

Where it is considered that a party to the appeal has behaved unreasonably the allegation and request for costs should be made before the conclusion of the inquiry rather than after the inquiry has closed. Circular 8/93 points out (Annex 5) that this enables the inspector to hear argument in relation to the claim. The inspector will also determine the request for costs unless the appeal is to be determined by the Secretary of State rather than by the inspector. In non-transferred cases, the inspector will report to the Secretary of State on the application and will make a recommendation on the matter. Post-inquiry claims for costs will not be entertained unless good reason can be shown for not making the claim at the inquiry stage, though the circular does not provide any examples of 'good reason'. Such claims will be unusual and will be conducted by written submissions rather than by a further appearance before the inspector. Parties are advised to keep such submissions brief and adhere to any time-limits which may be set.

In written representations cases, currently limited mainly to enforcement notice appeals, a request for costs should ordinarily be made to the Department of the Environment, Transport and the Regions (DETR) before the planning inspector carries out the site inspection. Since the parties should have exchanged their written representations by that stage it should then be clear what basis, if any, exists for an application for costs.

On a successful application the Secretary of State (or inspector in transferred cases) will award only those costs which are 'necessarily and reasonably incurred' (Annex 5, para 5) in relation to the proceedings. This excludes indirect costs, for example, those resulting from the fact that there has been a delay. The figure is not fixed administratively but is a matter for the parties to agree following a written submission of the details of the claim to the party against whom the award has been made. If agreement is not reached the party seeking payment can refer the matter to a Taxing Officer of the Supreme Court for determination. If resort to taxation is required, the parties will follow the procedure contained in a guidance note issued at the same time as the award of costs.

6.4 Partial award of costs

In some cases, an award of all costs necessarily and reasonably incurred will be inappropriate. Instead, a partial award can be made, for example, if the LPA have failed to substantiate one or more but not all the reasons for refusal of planning permission. Circular 8/93 advises that the costs of appealing against an unsubstantiated reason can be recovered (Annex 5, para 7). So far as unreasonable behaviour based on conduct is concerned, a partial award is also possible, for example, where an adjournment is necessitated, but limited to the extra expenses caused by the adjournment. For examples of partial awards, see *Planning Decisions Digest* (see Chapter 10).

6.5 Claims involving third parties

Almost all costs requests are made by one of the two principal parties to the appeal against the other party. Occasionally, a request will be made by or against a third party but it will require 'exceptional circumstances' for such a request to succeed. It is very unlikely that a claim based on the substance of the appeal will succeed but an allegation of unreasonable behaviour arising from conduct at the inquiry may be more successful if this leads to an unnecessary adjournment.

Where unreasonable behaviour causes the cancellation of an inquiry or the appellant withdraws the appeal too late for the inquiry to be cancelled, costs can be awarded in favour of third parties if they forewarned the LPA and appellant of their intention to appear at the inquiry before incurring expense in preparatory work. If the appellant and the LPA reach an agreement on the planning issues and the inquiry is thereby cancelled, third parties will not normally recover their costs.

6.6   Recovery of costs by the Secretary of State

Where a public local inquiry is arranged for the purposes of hearing any appeal to him under the 1990 Act, he is empowered by s 320 of that Act and s 250(4) of the Local Government Act 1972 to direct that the costs of the inquiry shall be paid by the LPA or any other party to the inquiry. This power was enlarged by s 42(2) of the Housing and Planning Act 1986 to enable the Secretary of State to recover the entire administrative costs of the inquiry including the 'general staff costs and overheads' of the DETR. By virtue of s 322A, these costs are recoverable even if the inquiry does not take place; an appellant who unreasonably makes a late withdrawal of his appeal therefore risks an award of costs against him.

Where the inquiry does take place any award of costs against the LPA or the appellant will be in accordance with a 'standard daily amount'. The relevant figure for these purposes is prescribed by statutory instrument, currently the Fees for Inquiries (Standard Daily Amount) (England) Regulations 2000 SI 2000/2307. These Regulations prescribe a standard daily amount of £561 in respect of inquiries opened in England on or after 1 October 2000, with an increase to £630 in respect of inquiries opened on or after 1 October 2001.

7 Forms and Precedents

A scheme of administration as complex as town and country planning inevitably generates a need for the use of official forms. Although many of the forms which are frequently used are prescribed by statutory instrument, most are not so prescribed and are devised at the discretion of individual local planning authorities (LPAs) or the Department of the Environment, Transport and the Regions (DETR). Using the same sequence of material which appears in Chapters 2 and 3, the following summarises the forms to be used and suggests further drafts, for example, of covering letters.

7.1 Application for planning permission

See para 2.5, 'Planning applications'. The following covering letter can be used and adapted to meet the needs of each possible type of planning application and the proposed form of development. Such forms as may be needed are listed at 2.5.2.

AN Other & Co, Solicitors, 14 Union Street, Worktown

Director of Development and Planning
Worktown District Council

Dear Sir

Town and Country Planning Act 1990 Application for Planning Permission: 2 Acacia Avenue, Worktown

We enclose four copies of an application for planning permission to change the use of the above property from use as a dwelling house to use as a nursing home. The proposed development also involves change of use of the curtilage of the property to provide car parking facilities. The enclosures are as follows:

(1) Four copies of application form.
(2) Four copies of site location plan.

(3) Four copies of drawings of the proposed development; these comprise plans of ground floor, first floor, and second floor, together with elevations drawings and car parking plan.

(4) Section 65 and General Development Procedure Order 1995, Art 7, certificate A.

(5) Fee of £190.

Yours faithfully

AN Other

Forms needed for an application for planning permission

Form	Source	Prescribed	Provision
Application for planning permission	LPA	No	
Notice to owner or tenant or newspaper notice on application for planning permission	LPA	Yes	GDPO 1995 Sched 2, Pt 1
Certificate of ownership	LPA	Yes	GDPO 1995 Sched 2, Pt 2

Certificate of ownership under Town and Country Planning (General Development Procedure) Order 1995

Practitioners should note that the prescribed forms of certificate of ownership specified in the Town and Country Planning (General Development Procedure) Order 1995 SI 1995/419 (GDPO 1995), Sched 2, Pt 2 are used with applications for planning permission and with appeals to the Secretary of State against refusal of planning permission, or grant subject to conditions. Appropriate deletions are therefore to be made when preparing the certificate for use with a planning application. In most instances, the applicant is the owner of the land and hence will submit Certificate A. In all cases, the Agricultural Holdings Certificate (see below) must also be submitted to the LPA.

Certificate under Art 7

Certificate A[1]

I certify that:

on the day 21 days before the date of the accompanying application/appeal* nobody, except the applicant/appellant*, was the owner[2] of any part of the land to which the application/appeal* relates.

Signed   On behalf of*

Date

or

Certificate B[1]

I certify that:

I have/The applicant has/The appellant has* given the requisite notice to everyone else who on the day 21 days before the date of the accompanying application/appeal, was the owner[2] of any part of the land to which the application/appeal* relates, as listed below.

Owner's name

Address at which notice was served

Date on which notice was served

Signed   On behalf of*

Date

or

Certificate C[1]

I certify that:

I/The applicant/The appellant* cannot issue a Certificate A or B in respect of the accompanying application/appeal*.

I have/The applicant has/The appellant has* given the requisite notice to the persons specified below, being persons who on the day 21 days before the date of the application/appeal*, were owners[2] of any part of the land to which the application/appeal* relates.

Owner's[2] name

Address at which notice was served

Date on which notice was served

I have/The applicant has/The appellant has★ taken all reasonable steps open to me/him/her★ to find out the names and addresses of the other owners[2] of the land, or of a part of it, but have been/has★ been unable to do so. These steps were as follows.[3]

Notice of the application/appeal★, as attached to this Certificate has been published in the[4] . . . . on[5] . . . .

Signed   On behalf of★

Date

or

Certificate D[1]

I certify that

I/The applicant/The appellant★ cannot issue a Certificate A in respect of the accompanying application/appeal★.

I/The applicant/The appellant★ have/has★ taken all reasonable steps open to me/him/her★ to find out the names and addresses of everyone else who, at the beginning of the period of 21 days beginning with the date of the application/appeal★, was the owner[2] of any part of the land to which the application/appeal★ relates, but have/has★ been unable to do so. These steps were as follows.[3]

Notice of the application/appeal★, as attached to this Certificate has been published in the[4] . . . . on[5] . . . .

Signed   On behalf of★

Date

★*Delete where appropriate*

Notes

1   This Certificate is for use with applications and appeals for planning permission (Arts 7 and 9(1) of the Order). One of Certificates A, B, C or D (or the appropriate certificate in the case of certain minerals applications) must be completed, together with the Agricultural Holdings Certificate.

2 'Owner' means a person having a freehold interest or a leasehold interest the unexpired term of which is not less then seven years, or in the case of development consisting of the winning and working of minerals a person entitled to an interest in a mineral in the land (other than oil, gas, coal, gold or silver).

3 Insert description of steps taken.

4 Insert name of newspaper circulating in the area where the land is situated.

5 Insert date of publication (which must not be earlier than the day 21 days before the date of the application or appeal).

Certificate under Art 7

Agricultural Holdings Certificate

Whichever is appropriate of the following alternatives must form part of Certificates A, B, C or D. If the applicant is the sole agricultural tenant he or she must delete the first alternative and insert 'not applicable' as the information required by the second alternative.

None of the land to which the application/appeal relates is, or is part of, an agricultural holding.

or

I have/The applicant has/The appellant has given the requisite notice to every person other than my/him/her*self who, on the day 21 days before the date of the application/appeal*, was a tenant of an agricultural holding on all or part of the land to which the application/appeal* relates, as follows:

Tenant's name

Address at which notice was served

Date on which notice was served

Signed   On behalf of*

Date

Delete where appropriate

1 This Certificate is for use with applications and appeals for planning permission (Arts 7 and 9(1) of the Order). One of certificates A, B, C or D (or the appropriate certificate in the case of certain minerals

applications) must be completed, together with the Agricultural Holdings Certificate.

7.2 Application for a certificate of lawfulness of proposed use or development

See para 2.6, 'Application for certificate of lawfulness of proposed use or development'. The form used is not presently prescribed though the Secretary of State is empowered by s 193 of the Town and Country Planning Act 1990 (the '1990 Act') to make appropriate provision for this procedure. The information required by the LPA will, however, reflect the requirements of Art 24 of the Town and Country Planning (General Permitted Development) Order 1995 SI 1995/418 (GPDO 1995). In the absence of a prescribed form, a suitable form will be provided by the LPA; an example appears below with specimen answers to the questions. In the example, the proposal in respect of which a certificate is being sought is in respect of use of rooms in a dwelling house by a medical practitioner. This is potentially a material change of use, though whether a material change of use would occur on implementation of the proposal is a matter of fact and degree for the LPA to decide.

Application for a certificate under s 192 of the Town and Country Planning Act 1990

Form	Source	Prescribed	Provision
Application for certificate of lawfulness of proposed use or present development	LPA	No (at present)	GDPO 1995, Art 24

Application for a certificate of lawfulness of proposed use or development under s 192 of the Town and Country Planning Act 1990

1A Name and address of applicant: *Dr R Hopeful, 38 Acacia Avenue, Worktown*

1B Name and address of agents (if form completed by agent):

AN Other & Co, Solicitors, 14 Union Street, Worktown, Planshire WT1 2BG

Tel No: *Worktown 342–8487 Fax: 342–8400*

2   (1) Nature of applicant's interest in the land, eg, owner, lessee, occupier

    (2) If you do not have an interest:

        (a) give name(s) and address(es) of anyone you know who has an interest in the land;

Owner:

        (b) state the nature of their interest (if known);

        (c) state whether they have been informed about this application. Yes/No

3   Address or exact location of the land to which the application relates: *38 Acacia Avenue, Worktown*

4   Has the proposal been started? Yes/No

5   If the proposal consists of, or includes, carrying out building or other operations give a detailed description of all★ such operations and attach such plans or drawings as are necessary to show their precise nature. (In the case of a proposed building the plans should indicate its precise siting and exact dimensions.) (★Includes the need to describe any proposal to alter or create a new access, lay out a new street, construct any associated hardstandings, means of enclosure or means of draining the land/buildings)

6   If the proposal relates to a change of the use of the land or building(s):

    (1) Give a full description of the scale and nature of the proposed use, including the processes to be carried on, any machinery to be installed, and the hours the proposed use will be carried on

        (1) The proposed future use of this property is as a dwelling house in which two ground floor rooms are to be used by the applicant during specified hours for the purpose of general medical practice. The rooms affected are noted on the enclosed drawing

        (2) The room marked A on the plan is to be used for consulting purposes, while the room marked B on the plan is for the use of patients awaiting consultation

        (3) Surgery hours are to be between 10.00 am and 12.30 pm, Monday to Saturday; and between 5.00 pm and 6.30 pm, Monday to Friday. It is anticipated that approximately 20 patients will call at the premises per day during the first year of practice, but that approximately 30 patients can be expected to call daily in subsequent years. The number of patients calling daily should stabilise at the end of the second year of practice. The applicant's private patients (if any) will call during the stated surgery hours and are included in the estimates given. All patients will call by appointment only

        (4) Outside surgery hours the rooms marked A and B are to be used by the applicant as a study and as a lounge, respectively. It will be observed therefore that neither room is to be used exclusively for the purposes of medical practice

        (5) The applicant will engage the services of a receptionist who will use a desk and telephone situated in the waiting room/lounge. The receptionist will attend on a part time basis for between two and three hours in the morning and for a similar period in the evening

> *(6) Patients' medical records will be stored in the waiting room/lounge.*
>
> *(7) Medical supplies and the applicant's professional apparatus will be stored in the proposed consulting room/study*
>
> *(Continue on a separate sheet if necessary)*

(2) fully describe the existing use or last known use, with the date when this use ceased

Dwelling house

7   Briefly explain why you consider the existing, or last, use of the land is lawful, or why you consider that any existing buildings which it is proposed to alter or extend are lawful. (You can use s 11 of this application to state your case more fully.) Specify the supporting documentary evidence (such as planning permission) which accompanies this application

Planning permission for construction of the dwelling house was granted by Worktown District Council on 3rd April 1985, ref W/APP/850219

8   If you consider the existing, or last, use is within a 'use class' in the Town and Country Planning (Use Classes) Order 1987, state which one

Class C3

9   If you consider the proposed use is within a 'use class' in the Town and Country Planning (Use Classes) Order 1987, state which one

Not applicable

10 Is the proposed operation or use temporary or permanent?

Permanent

If temporary, give details

11 State why you consider that a Lawful Development Certificate should be granted for this proposal

Although the proposal involves a change of use, it is not a material change of use within s 55(1) of the Town and Country Planning Act 1990

(Continue on a separate sheet if necessary)

12 List here all the documents, drawings or plans which accompany this application (to include a copy of an OS-based plan showing boundary of site edged in red)

Site location plan

Internal layout plan showing ground and first floors

I/We hereby apply for a lawful use or development certificate under s 192 of the 1990 Act in respect of the existing use, operations or activity described in this application and the documents, drawings and plans which accompany it. I/We enclose the appropriate fee of £95

Signed *AN Other & Co*   Date *31st March 2001*

On behalf of *Dr R Hopeful*

(Insert name of applicant if signed by an agent)

A suitable covering letter for this type of application is as follows. This can be adapted as necessary to meet the needs of other proposals.

AN Other & Co, Solicitors, 14 Union Street, Worktown

Director of Development and Planning

Worktown District Council

Dear Sir

Application for Certificate of Lawfulness of Proposed Use or Development under the Town and Country Planning Act 1990, s 192: 38 Acacia Avenue, Worktown

I enclose an application for a certificate under s 192 of the Town and Country Planning Act 1990 on behalf of my client, Dr R Hopeful, of the above address. The application concerns the proposed use of two ground floors rooms in the above dwelling house for general medical practice. The enclosures are as follows:

(1) four copies of application form with statement of particulars of proposed use attached;

(2) four copies of site location plan;

(3) four copies of plans showing ground and first floors.

Although the Town and Country Planning (General Development Procedure) Order 1995 does not require additional copies of the application to be submitted, We have, nevertheless, enclosed three additional copies for your convenience.

Yours faithfully

AN Other & Co

7.3 Application for a certificate of lawfulness of existing use of development

See para 2.7, 'Application for a certificate of lawfulness of existing use or development'. An application for a certificate of lawfulness of existing use of development (or 'CLEUD') is administratively subject to similar considerations to the certificate of lawfulness of proposed use or development (or 'CLOPUD'). Thus, there is no prescribed form of application but the requirements of Art 24 of the GDPO 1995 apply. A suitable form of application will be provided by the LPA. In the following example, the applicant is seeking a CLEUD in circumstances where the local planning authority are considering taking enforcement action in respect of the use of a dwelling house which was originally used for the purpose of occupation by one family but which has been used for the purposes of six bedsitting rooms with use of common parts. It is accepted by the parties that there is no relevant grant of planning permission in existence authorising the relevant change of use. The issue is whether the use has subsisted for at least 10 years and is therefore a lawful use.

Application for a certificate of lawfulness of existing use or development under s 191 of the Town and Country Planning Act 1990

1A Name and address of applicant: *IC Money, 7 Cash Lane, Worktown*

1B Name and address of agent (if form completed by agent):

AN Other & Co, Solicitors, 14 Union Street, Worktown

Tel No: *Worktown 342 8487 Fax: 342–8400*

2 (1) Nature of applicant's interest in the land, eg, owner, lessee occupier:

Owner

(2) If you do not have an interest:

(a) give name(s) and address(es) of anyone you know who has an interest in the land;

(b) state the nature of their interest (if known);

(c) state whether they have been informed of this application. Yes/No

3 Address or exact location of the land to which this application relates:

20 Flatland Hill Road, Worktown

Describe here and enclose a copy of an OS-based plan showing the boundary of the land edged in red

See OS map section AB1234

4 This application is in respect of:

an existing use

an existing operation

an existing use, operation or activity in breach of a condition

(tick relevant box)

being a use, operation or activity subsisting on the date of this application

5 If there is more than one subsisting use of, or operation or activity on, the land at the date of this application, describe fully each of them and, where appropriate, show to which part of the land each use, operation or activity relates

Not applicable – this application relates to one use only

6   When was the use or activity begun, or the operation substantially completed?

September 1988

7   Under what grounds is the certificate sought?

(delete those which are not applicable)

   (1) The use began more than ten years before the date of this application; or

   (2) The use, operation or activity in breach of condition began more than ten years before the date of this application; or

   (3) The use began within the last ten years, as a result of a change of us not requiring planning permission, and there has not been a change of use requiring planning permission in the last ten years;

   (4) The operations were substantially completed more than four years before the date of this application;

   (5) The use as a single dwelling house began more than four years before the date of this application;

   (6) Other – specify (this might include claims that the change of use or operation was not development, or that it benefitted from planning permission granted under the 1990 Act or the General Permitted Development Order 1995 or previous Orders).

   (Note – ground (1) is the relevant ground in this example)

8   If a certificate is sought for a use, operation or activity in breach of a condition or limitation, specify the condition or limitation which has not been complied with, and attach a copy of the relevant planning permission

Not applicable – the application relates to a change of use without planning permission

9   Give any additional information you consider necessary to substantiate your claim

For the applicant's statement of reasons why a Certificate of Lawfulness of Existing Use should be granted see attachment

10 List here all the documents, drawings or plans which accompany this application

   (1) *Site location plan*

   (2) *Land Registry Office Copy entries*

   (3) *Accounts in respect of furnished lettings of 20 Flatland Hill Road, Worktown from 1991 to 2000*

   (4) *Statement of CD (resident since 1988)*

   (5) *Copies of applicants banking counterfoils and handwritten notes*

11 We hereby apply for a certificate of lawful use or development under section 191 of the Town and Country Planning Act 1990. We enclose the appropriate fee of £190

Signed *AN Other & Co*   date   *31st March 2001*

On behalf of   *IC Money*

(insert name of applicant if signed by an agent)

Applicant's Statement of Reasons why a CLEUD should be granted

1. *Mr IC Money purchased 20 Flatland Hill Road on 1 March 1988. At that time the property comprised a single family dwelling house*

2. *On 11 September 1988 the applicant let one of the rooms to AB under an oral agreement. A banking counterfoil is the only available evidence of the commencement of this tenancy. On the reverse of the counterfoil the applicant has written 'First payment of rent for room 4 from AB'*

3. *On 13 September 1988 the applicant sought and obtained Certificates of Fair Rent in respect of all six bed-sitting rooms*

4. *On 15 September 1988 two bedsitting rooms were let to CD and EF. These were also oral agreements. The evidence of these lettings is limited to banking counterfoils and handwritten notes made by the applicant. Further lettings on oral tenancies were made in respect of all other rooms involving various tenants. Occupation of all the rooms was complete by 2 November 1988. There is some corroborative evidence available from the Council's own records including two applications for a Rent Allowance made in 1989*

5. *Subsequently all the rooms were occupied pursuant to written agreements, the first of which is dated 12 February 1991. One of the first tenants CD, is still resident in the property pursuant to a written agreement dated 24 April 1991. He has provided a statement in support of this application confirming that all the rooms were occupied no later than the end of 1988*

6. *The applicant instructed an accountant in May 1991 to prepare his accounts. The accounts are complete and cover the period 1991 to 2000. They demonstrate, subject to an occasional vacancy, virtually full occupancy of the six bedsitting rooms throughout the relevant period*

7. *The above information clearly demonstrates that the present use of the property commenced more than 10 years ago and has continued since commencement*

A suitable covering letter for this type of application is as follows

AN Other & Co, Solicitors, 14 Union Street, Worktown

Director of Development and Planning

Worktown District Council

Dear Sir

Application for a Certificate of Lawfulness of Existing Use or Development under the Town and Country Planning Act 1990, s 191: 20 Flatland Hill Road, Worktown

We enclose an application for a certificate under s 191 of the Town and Country Planning Act 1990 on behalf of our client Mr IC Money of 'Packemin' Rich Road, Worktown. The application concerns the use of a dwelling house as six bedsitting rooms. The relevant rooms were all occupied more than ten years ago and therefore we now seek the appropriate certificate. Documentation in support of the application is enclosed and is listed at para 10 of the application.

Yours faithfully,

AN Other & Co

7.4 Application for listed building or conservation area consent

See para 2.8, 'Application for listed building consent or conservation area consent'. Some of the forms which are relevant to an application for listed building or conservation area consent are prescribed by the Planning (Listed Buildings and Conservation Areas) Regulations 1990 SI 1990/1519 (the '1990 Regulations'). The form of application itself is not, however, prescribed. References below are to the 1990 regulations; such forms as are needed are listed on p 38.

Forms needed for application for listed building or conservation area consent (see Chapter 2).

Form	Source	Prescribed	Provision
Application for listed building or conservation area consent	LPA	No	—
Certificates of ownership A–D	LPA	Yes	1990 Regs, Sched 2, Pt 1
Notice for service on owners (Certificate B case)	Prepare in office	Yes	1990 Regs Sched 2, Pt ll
Newspaper notice (Certificate C and D cases)	Prepare in office	Yes	1990 Regs, Sched 2, Pt ll

In those cases in which Certificate B is required to be submitted by the applicant, the certificate must state that notice has been given to other owners specifying their names, addresses and the dates of service. Notice served on such persons must be in the form specified by Sched 2, Pt II.

Schedule 2 to the Planning (Listed Buildings and Conservation Areas) Regulations 1990

PART I

Certificate A*

I hereby certify that no person other than [myself] [the applicant] [the appellant]* was the owner[1] of any of the building to which the [application] [appeal]* relates at the beginning of the period of 21 days ending with the date of the accompanying [application] [appeal]*

or

Certificate B*

I hereby certify that:

[I have] [The applicant has] [The appellant has]* given the requisite notice to all the persons other than [myself] [the applicant] [the appellant]* who, at the beginning of the period of 21 days ending with the date of the accompanying [application] [appeal]*, were owners[1] of the building to which the [application] [appeal]* relates

Name of owner

Address

Date of service of notice

or

Certificate C*

I hereby certify that:

(1) [I am] [The applicant is] [The appellant is]* unable to issue a certificate in accordance with either sub-paragraph (a) or sub-paragraph (b) of reg 6(1) of the Planning (Listed Buildings and Conservation Areas) Regulations 1990 in respect of the accompanying [application] [appeal]* dated

(2) I have] [The applicant has] [The appellant has]* given the requisite notice to the following persons other than [myself] [the applicant] [the appellant]* who, at the beginning of the period of 21 days ending with the date of the [application] [appeal]*, were owners[1] of the building to which the [application] [appeal] relates

Name of owner

Address

Date of service of notice

(3) [I have] [the applicant has] [the appellant has]★ taken the steps listed below, being steps reasonably open to [me] [him]★ to ascertain the names and addresses of the other owners[1] of the building and [have] [has]★ been unable to do so:[2]

(4) Notice of the [application] [appeal]★ as set out below has been published in the[3] . . . . .on[4] . . . .

Copy of notice as published

or

Certificate D*

I hereby certify that:

(1) [I am] [the applicant is] [The appellant is]★ unable to issue a certificate in accordance with sub-paragraph (a) of reg 6(1) of the Planning (Listed Building and Conservation Areas) Regulations 1990 in respect of the accompanying [application] [appeal]★ dated ... and [have] [has]★ taken the steps listed below, being steps open to [me] [him]★ to ascertain the names and addresses of all the persons other than [myself] [himself]★ who, at the beginning of the period of 21 days ending with the date of the [application] [appeal]★ relates and [have] [had] been unable to do so:[2]

(2) Notice of the [application] [appeal]★ as set out below has been published

in the[3] . . . . .on[4] . . . .

Copy of the notice as published

Signed   Date

[on behalf of]★

★   *Delete where inappropriate*

Notes

1 'Owner' means a person having a freehold interest or a leasehold interest of which not less than seven years remain unexpired.

2 Insert descriptions of steps taken.

3 Insert name of local newspaper circulating in the locality in which the land is situated.

4 Insert date of publication (which must not be earlier than 20 days before the application or appeal).

PART II

Notice for service on individuals

Proposal for [demolishing] [altering] [extending] [varying or discharging conditions]★[1]

TAKE NOTICE that application is being made to the[2] . . . . . . Council by[3] . . . . for [listed building consent] [conservation area consent] [variation or discharge of conditions]★[4]

If you wish to make representations about the application, you should make them in writing, not later than[5] . . . . .to the Council at[6]

Signed

[on behalf of   ]★

Date

Notice for publication in local newspapers where not all the owners are known, pursuant to reg 6(2) of the Planning (Listed Buildings and Conservation Areas) Regulations 1990

Proposal for [demolishing] [altering] [extending] [varying or discharging conditions]★[1]

Notice is hereby given that application is being made to the[2] . . . . Council by[3] . . . . for [listed building consent] [conservation area consent] [variation or discharge of conditions]★[4] Any owner of the building (namely a freeholder, or a leaseholder entitled to an unexpired term of at least seven years) who wishes to make representations to the above-mentioned Council about the application should make them in writing not later than[5] . . . .

to the Council at[6]

Signed

[on behalf of   ]★

Date

★   *Delete where inappropriate*

Notes

1   Insert name, address or location of building with sufficient precision to ensure identification of it.

2   Insert name of council.

3   Insert name of applicant.

4   Insert description of proposed works and name, address or location of building, or in the case of an application to vary or discharge conditions, insert description of the proposed variation or discharge.

5   Insert date not less than 20 days later than the date on which the notice is served or published.

6   Insert address of council.

In those cases in which Certificates C or D are required to be submitted by the applicant, a statement must also be included confirming that a notice in a local newspaper has been published in the form required by Sched 2, Pt II.

The following covering letter can be used to make an application for consent for the demolition of a listed building or a building contained within a conservation area. This can be adapted as occasion requires.

AN Other & Co, Solicitors, 14 Union Street, Worktown

Director of Development and Planning

Worktown District Council

Dear Sir

Planning (Listed Buildings and Conservation Areas) Act 1990 Application for Listed Building Consent: 37 Hanover Street, Worktown.

We enclose three copies of an application for listed building consent for the demolition of the above property. It is proposed to redevelop the site of this building and an application for planning permission is being submitted simultaneously with this application. It is understood from Annex B to PPG 15 that the application should be made in triplicate. The enclosures are therefore as follows:

(1) three copies of application form;

(2) three copies of site location plan;

(3) Certificate A as prescribed by the Planning (Listed Buildings and Conservation Areas) Regulations 1990;

(4) two sets of floor plans and drawings showing the structure before the proposed works and the altered structure [or new development to replace the building] after the proposed works have been carried out;

(5) photographs showing the architectural details of the building, as recommended by Annex B to Planning Policy Guidance Note 15.

Yours faithfully

AN Other & Co

7.5 Opposing development proposals

See para 2.9, 'Opposing development proposals'. A prescribed form is in use for the purpose of notification by LPAs of adjoining owners of development proposals, whether by personal notice, newspaper notification or site notice; the form of notice is as specified by Art 8 of and Sched 3 to the GDPO 1995. There is no formal requirement, other than to communicate in writing, for the purposes of making an objection to such proposals. An example is now given of a notice from the LPA informing a neighbour of a proposed development of land for a floodlit hard-surfaced sports playing area in circumstances where the developer has carried out a similar development on adjacent land. As illustrated below, the content of the letter of objection will depend on the proposed development, the provisions of the development plan, the relevant planning history, if any, together with any points of a planning nature (material considerations) which demonstrate why the application should be refused by the LPA.

Town and Country Planning (General Development Procedure) Order 1995: Notice under Art 8

(To be published in a newspaper, displayed on or near the site, or served on owners and/or occupiers of adjoining land.)

> Proposed development at (a) *Land on the north side of Acacia Avenue, Worktown (adjacent to Worktown Sports Club).*
>
> I give notice that (b) *Worktown Leisure Limited* is applying to the (c) *Worktown District Council* for planning permission to (d) *construct a hard-surfaced sports playing area with floodlighting on land adjacent to Worktown Sports Club.*
>
> The proposed development does not accord with the provisions of the development plan in force in the area in which the land to which the application relates is situated.*
>
> Members of the public may inspect copies of:
>
> * the application;
>
> * the plans;
>
> * and other documents submitted with it
>
> at (e) *The Department of Development and Planning, The Town Hall, Victoria Road, Worktown* during all reasonable hours until (f) date.

Anyone who wishes to make representations about this application should write to: the Council at (g) The Department of Development and Planning, The Town Hall, Victoria Road, Worktown

by (f) date

Signed   On behalf of Worktown District Council

Dated

Delete where inappropriate

Insert:

(a) address or location of the proposed development;

(b) applicant's name;

(c) name of Council;

(d) description of the proposed development;

(e) address at which the application may be inspected;

(f) date giving a period of 21 days, beginning with the date when the notice is first displayed on or near the site or served on an owner and/or occupier of adjoining land, or a period of 14 days, beginning with the date when the notice is published in a newspaper (as the case may be);

(g) address of Council.

A specimen reply to this notice would be as follows:

AN Other & Co, Solicitors, 14 Union Street, Worktown

Director of Development and Planning
Worktown District Council
Town Hall
Victoria Road
Worktown

Dear Sir

Town and Country Planning Act 1990

Proposed Development at: Land on the north side of Acacia Avenue, Worktown (adjacent to Worktown Sports Club)

Your notice dated . . . . . . concerning the above proposal and addressed to the owner occupier of 62 Acacia Avenue has been passed to us by our client Mr John Smith. In your notice an invitation was made to submit representations to the Council as the local planning authority for consideration by the Planning Committee. We will be obliged if you will treat this letter as our client's response to your notice. Under the provisions of the current Development Plan the land in question is not identified for use for any particular purpose but the application site in shown contained within a predominately residential area.

Reference to the provisions of the Development Plan (Policy C 11) shows that the Local Planning Authority consider that the existing provision of such pitches within the Worktown area is sufficient to meet demand and also acknowledges the advice contained in PPG 17 (Sport and Recreation) that floodlighting will normally require planning permission. It is submitted that the planning merits clearly indicate that this application should be refused.

The site which is the subject of the application is directly opposite my client's residence. My client is therefore very concerned about this proposed development and, for reasons which appear below, wishes to object to it in the strongest possible terms. It is submitted that the proposed development, if permitted, would be detrimental to the amenity of this predominantly residential area.

This submission is based on my client's complaint of existing loss of amenity due to the use currently being made of a similar playing area adjacent to the site of the proposed development, in respect of which planning permission was granted to the applicant on 4 January 1993. The implementation of that grant of planning permission has not only caused a loss of visual amenity but is also the source of frequent and unpleasant noise disturbance emanating from players of football and supporting spectators. This disturbance has been of such a degree of discomfort that my client has found it necessary to complain to the developer.

Disturbance is also caused by visitors' cars since there is no public transport provision available in the immediate area.

Relevant vehicle movements have increased in recent years and hence further development at this site would only exacerbate this problem.

Further concerns are raised by the present proposal in having regard to the proposed floodlighting. If implemented, this aspect of the proposal would cause further visual intrusion due to the unsightly structures needed for the floodlighting and also due to the intense light which they generate when operational.

For these reasons it is submitted that the application for planning permission for the development which is now being proposed should be refused.

Yours faithfully

AN Other & Co

8 Criminal Offences and Penalties

The purpose of this chapter is to make provision for tables giving details of the main criminal offences which are associated with the town and country planning legislation. Numerous offences have been created, some involving a possible penalty of imprisonment, though the majority are punishable only by imposition of a fine. In many cases, the offence is triable either way and can lead to imposition of an unlimited fine if conviction is obtained in the Crown Court.

Not all the offences of which developers need to be aware are contained in the Town and Country Planning Act 1990 (the '1990 Act'); other offences, for example, under the Planning (Listed Buildings and Conservation Areas) Act 1990 or earlier legislation such as the Caravan Sites and Control of Development Act 1960, are considered separately below.

8.1 Summary only and triable either way offences

Since many of the offences created by town and country planning legislation are triable either way, the relevant maximum penalties are normally as specified in the provision concerned. Offences which are summary only are usually subject to the standard scale introduced by s 37 of the Criminal Justice Act 1982. Penalties under the standard scale were revised by the Criminal Justice Act 1991 with effect from 1 October 1992. The standard scale is presently as follows:

Summary only offences

Level on standard scale	Maximum fine
	£
1	200
2	500
3	1,000
4	2,500
5	5,000

In the table which appears below a number of references are made to the appropriate level on the standard scale. In the case of some offences, however, the maximum fine is inserted in figures, thus, indicating that the offence is triable either way.

Table of criminal offences under the Town and Country Planning Act 1990

Nature of offence	Provision	Magistrates' court	Crown Court
Submission of false or misleading certificate in support of planning application	65(6)	Level 5	—
Failure to comply with requirements of a planning contravention notice	171D(1) and (4)	Level 3	—
Submission of false or misleading information in response to a planning contravention notice	171D(5) and (6)	Level 5	—
Failure to comply with requirements of a breach of condition notice	187A(8) and (12)	Level 3	—
Second or subsequent conviction	187A(10) and (12)	Level 3	—
Failure to comply with requirements of an enforcement notice	179(2) and (8)	£20,000 fine	unlimited fine
Second or subsequent conviction	179(6) and (8)	£20,000 fine	unlimited fine

Nature of offence	Provision	Magistrates' court	Crown Court
Failure to comply with requirements of a stop notice	187(1) and (2)	£20,000 fine	unlimited fine
Second or subsequent conviction	187(1A) and (2)	£20,000 fine	unlimited fine
Knowingly or recklessly making a false or misleading statement to procure a certificate of lawfulness of existing use or development or a certificate of lawfulness of proposed use or development	194(1) and (2)	Level 5	2 years' imprisonment or unlimited fine (or both)
Contravention of a tree preservation order	210(1) and (2)	£20,000 fine	unlimited fine
Contravention of a 'waste land' notice	216(2)	Level 3	—
Second or subsequent conviction	216(6)	one-10th of Level 3 per day fine	—
Failure to comply with discontinuance order, or order requiring removal of buildings or works	189(1) and (3)	£5,000 fine	unlimited fine
Contravention of Advertisement Regs 1992	224(3)	Level 3	—
Second or subsequent conviction	224(3)	one-10th of Level 3 per day fine	—
Breach of listed building control	9(4)★	6 months' imprisonment or £20,000 fine (or both)	2 years' imprisonment or unlimited fine (or both)
Failure to comply with requirements of a listed building enforcement notice	43(5)★	£20,000 fine	unlimited fine
Second or subsequent conviction	43(5)★	£20,000 fine	unlimited fine
Breach of hazardous substance control	23(4)★★	£20,000 fine	unlimited fine

Nature of offence	Provision	Magistrates' court	Crown Court
Breach of conservation area control	74(3)★	6 months' imprisonment or £20,000 fine (or both)	2 years' imprisonment or unlimited fine (or both)
Failure to provide information concerning interests in land after service of notice under s 330	330(4)	Level 3	—
Submission of false information in response to a s 330 notice	330(5)	Level 5	2 years' imprisonment or unlimited fine (or both)

★Planning (Listed Buildings and Conservation Areas) Act 1990
★★Planning (Hazardous Substances) Act 1990

8.2 Offences arising under other relevant legislation

8.2.1 Failure to obtain relevant consents

It was noted in para 2.4, 'Determining whether other consents are required', that a consent other than planning permission is required in certain cases. Two of the four cases mentioned in that paragraph (those which relate to consent required under a tree preservation order and to hazardous substances consent) arise by virtue of the provisions of the 1990 Act and the Planning (Hazardous Substances) Act 1990, respectively. The penalties which are associated with failure to comply with those controls have therefore been noted in the above table. Of the remaining two cases (concerning scheduled monument consent and the requirement for a caravan site licence), the table at the end of this chapter summarises the penalties involved.

8.2.2 Failure to give relevant notifications

This paragraph provides a suitable opportunity in which to summarise two other controls over development which apply in certain cases depending on the location of the land concerned. Neither of these controls require the developer to seek a specific consent (other than planning permission if development is involved) to enable the proposal to be implemented; rather they operate in such a way as to require notification of proposals to be given to a statutory body. Both of these controls arise from the designation of areas for the specific purposes which appear below:

(a) Sites of Special Scientific Interest (SSSIs)

If the Nature Conservancy Council for England (or, in Wales, the Countryside Council for Wales) believe that any land is of special interest by reason of its flora, fauna, geological or physiographical features they must notify the local planning authority (LPA), Secretary of State and owners and occupiers pursuant to s 28 of the Wildlife and Countryside Act 1981. The notification specifies what operations are likely to damage the flora, fauna, etc, for example, ploughing or forestry as well as development within the meaning of the 1990 Act. If it is proposed to carry out any such operations, four months' notice must be given to the relevant Council during which specific consent can be obtained or an agreement can be made under which payments are made by the relevant Council for maintaining the land in its existing condition. There are about 2,000 such sites in England and Wales. Failure to give notice to the Council is an offence.

(b) Areas of Archaeological Importance (AAIs)

Redevelopment of sites principally in urban areas may be the subject of grant by the developer of compulsory archaeological research facilities for up to four-and-a-half months if the area has been designated by the Secretary of State or the LPA as one of archaeological importance under s 33 of the Ancient Monuments and Archaeological Areas Act 1979. If a developer wishes to carry out any operation which will involve flooding or tipping or will 'disturb the ground' s 35 requires service of an 'operations notice' on the LPA who will then notify the archaeological investigating authority (a body appointed by the Secretary of State). The archaeological investigating authority has four weeks in which it may give notice of intention to investigate the site. Designations currently exist in the central areas of Berwick-upon-Tweed, Canterbury, Chester, Colchester, Exeter, Gloucester, Hereford, Lincoln, Oxford and York. Failure to serve an operations notice when required is an offence.

The penalties for the above offences may be summarised as shown in the following table:

Nature of offence	Statutory provision	Magistrates' court	Crown Court
Breach of scheduled monument control	Ancient Monuments and Archaeological Areas Act 1979, s 2(10)	£5,000 fine	unlimited fine
Destruction of or damage to a protected monument	1979 Act, s 28(4)	6 months' imprisonment or £5,000 fine (or both)	2 years' imprisonment or unlimited fine (or both)
Use of land as a caravan site for human habitation without a site licence	Caravan Sites and Control of Development Act 1960, s 1(2)	Level 4	—
Second or subsequent conviction	1960 Act, s 1(2)	Level 4	—
Failure to comply with a condition attached to a site licence	1960 Act, s 9(1)	Level 4	—
Second or subsequent conviction	1960 Act, s 9(1)	Level 4	—
Failure to notify Nature Conservancy Council of proposed operations in an SSSI	Wildlife and Countryside Act 1981, s 28(7)	Level 4	—
Failure to serve operations notice on LPA in an AAI	Ancient Monuments and Archaeological Areas Act 1979, s 35(9)	£5,000 fine	unlimited fine

9 Answers to Common Questions

Many of the common questions which are raised have been dealt with in the text of the previous chapters. The following matters may, nevertheless, be of interest.

(a) Is it always necessary to submit three additional copies of all applications to the local planning authority?

This can be deduced from the Town and Country Planning (General Development Procedure) Order 1995 SI 1995/419 or other instrument regulating the application in question. Although in some instances no legal requirement is imposed to submit additional copies, for example, for an application for a certificate of lawfulness of proposed use or development under s 192 of the Town and Country Planning Act ('the 1990 Act'), the local planning authority (LPA) will often take the view that additional copies should be submitted. Also, some planning officers are not aware that additional copies are not always required. To avoid delays it is advisable to submit three additional copies from the outset. Note, however, that in the case of an application for express consent for the display of an advertisement, reg 9(3) of the Town and Country Planning (Control of Advertisements) Regulations 1992 requires two additional copies of the application to be submitted.

(b) If I wish to make an appeal against refusal of planning permission, or against the issue of an enforcement notice, to be the subject of a public local inquiry, do I risk an award of costs if I lose the appeal and the inspector considers that the appeal could have been disposed of by means of written representations?

No. Annex 2, para 1 to Department of the Environment Circular 8/93 advises that costs are not awarded simply because an oral hearing has been requested. Each party has the right under s 79 of the 1990 Act to an oral hearing. It is not unreasonable behaviour to exercise this statutory right even if the appeal was suitable for the written representations method.

(c) What are my prospects of success on appeal to the Secretary of State from an adverse decision by the LPA?

Statistically, about one in three planning appeals are successful. Allowing for a proportion of poorly presented appeals and those with remote prospects of success, the success rate for serious well prepared appeals is more of the order of 40%.

(d) If more than eight weeks elapse from submission of the application but the LPA subsequently issue a grant of planning permission, is it safe to act on it?

Although failure to reach a decision within the eight weeks period (or any longer period agreed in writing) means that the applicant may proceed to appeal to the Secretary of State (s 79(2) of the 1990 Act), this only operates to enable the applicant to implement the right of appeal granted by s 78. If planning permission is granted out of time but accepted and acted upon by the applicant it will be a valid grant (*James v Minister of Housing and Local Government* [1966] 1 WLR 135). Note, however, that if an appeal is made arising from the deemed refusal of the application for planning permission, the LPA will no longer have jurisdiction in respect of the application. For this reason, developers sometimes submit two identical applications and make an appeal in respect of one deemed refusal, thus, leaving the LPA with jurisdiction to determine the other application out of time.

(e) Is application for outline planning permission relevant to a proposed material change of use?

No. Application for a proposed material change of use is always for a grant of full planning permission.

(f) Does my client need to own the land before he can make an application?

No. Anyone may make an application for planning permission though a non-owner will need to notify owners of the making of the application.

(g) Is there a right of appeal against a grant of planning permission?

No. Appeal is only available in respect of refusal or a grant subject to conditions. An aggrieved neighbour must rely on judicial review to quash a decision of the LPA or apply to the High Court under s 288 of the 1990 Act if permission is granted by the Secretary of State.

(h) Who can appeal to the Secretary of State against a planning decision?

Only the original applicant; a subsequent owner of the land does not take the land together with any outstanding appeal rights.

(i) Is it an offence to develop land without planning permission?

No. It is, however, an offence to fail to comply with the requirements of an enforcement notice, breach of condition notice or stop notice. It is also an offence to fail to comply with any requirement of a planning contravention notice.

(j) If I exercise my right to inspect the content of the planning register or other registers maintained by the LPA am I allowed to take copies of the contents?

Copies of documents issued by the LPA can be taken away, for example, of grants or refusal of planning permission, or of enforcement notices. Documents submitted by other parties can also be copied since this material is subject to s 47 of the Copyright Act 1988 which authorises the copying of material which is required to be made available for public inspection.

(k) How long must I realistically wait for a decision on an application for planning permission?

About 60% of all applications are determined within the required eight week period. A further 25% are determined within the next four weeks.

10 Further Reading

The planning law library has become substantial in recent years; this reflects the growth of the primary source material and the consequent willingness on the part of publishers to commission books which deal with individual well-defined areas of the subject, as well as texts which seek to encompass 'planning law' as a whole. The following comprises a selection of texts which are in the latter category:

Grant, M, *The Encyclopedia of Planning Law and Practice*, 1959, London: Sweet & Maxwell

> This seven-volume looseleaf work is the practitioner's companion. It is regularly updated and includes high quality annotations prepared by the editor.

Heap, D, *An Outline of Planning Law*, 11th edn, 1996, London: Sweet & Maxwell

> This book has grown by editions to some 600 pages. Its main merit is that it has something to say about virtually every provision in the town and country planning legislation and is therefore very useful in identifying relevant law and providing a summary of relevant procedure.

Telling, AE and Duxbury, RMC, *Planning Law and Procedure,* 10th edn, 1996, London: Butterworths

> This long established work is less extensive than those listed above but has the merit of having been written in a lucid style. Very suitable for introductory purposes as well as for use by more experienced practitioners.

The following are examples of practical handbooks which will often give access to or facilitate swift solutions to a planning law or practice question:

Brand, CM and Williams, DW, *Planning Law for Conveyancers*, 4th edn, 1996, London: FT Law and Tax

Many questions of planning law are raised during conveyancing transactions. This book explains their relevance and significance.

Greenwood, B *et al*, *Butterworths Planning Law Service*, 1995, London: Butterworths

A one-volume looseleaf work which combines discussion of the legislation with a precedent service. The emphasis is on effective discharge of clients' instructions.

Greenwood, B, *Butterworths Planning Law Handbook*, 5th edn, 2000, London: Butterworths

This contains the 'raw' text of legislation, both primary and secondary.

Purdue, M and Fraser, V, *Planning Decisions Digest*, 2nd edn, 1992, London: Sweet & Maxwell

A useful source book which lists by reference to section numbers all the judicial and ministerial decisions which have been made under the main provisions of the Town and Country Planning Acts. Each entry contains a brief note of the case, thus, enabling the reader to determine its relevance and hence refer, if necessary to the report.

Tromans, S and Turrall-Clarke, R, *Planning Law, Practice and Precedents*, 1991, London: Sweet & Maxwell

A practitioner's work in looseleaf form which gives access to a wide range of precedent material.

The following texts deal with selected aspects of planning law and practice.

Bourne, F, *Enforcement of Planning Control*, 1992, London: Sweet & Maxwell

Emphasising the practical aspects, this book is a very useful aid in the conduct of enforcement proceedings.

Millichap, D, *The Effective Enforcement of Planning Controls*, 1991, London: Butterworths

This book unravels the legal complexities of enforcement proceedings and explains the statutory provisions and the attendant substantial body of case law.

Suddards, R and Hargreaves, P, *Listed Buildings*, 3rd edn, 1996, London: Sweet & Maxwell

This book is a leading text on conservation and preservation of the built environment.

Mynors, C, *Listed Buildings, Conservation Areas and Monuments*, 3rd edn, 1998, London: Sweet & Maxwell

A first class work which brings together the practical knowledge and experience gained by the author both as a barrister and, in an earlier part of his career, as a conservation officer.

Mynors, C, *Planning Control and the Display of Advertisements*, 1992, London: Sweet & Maxwell

This book provides an exhaustive account of the law relevant to the display of advertisements by providing a detailed commentary on the relevant legislation and policy guidance.

Journals and specialist reports

Journal of Planning and Environment Law (JPL), London: Sweet & Maxwell

This monthly journal is the main periodical and includes not only law reports and planning appeal decisions but also advice on recent statutory instruments and circulars.

Property, Planning and Compensation Reports (P & CR), London: Sweet & Maxwell

Issued bi-monthly, this journal contains the text of the principal judicial decisions.

Planning Appeal Decisions (PAD), London: Sweet & Maxwell

This series commenced in 1986. Issued bi-monthly, it facilitates access for practitioners to ministerial decisions.

Estates Gazette (EG), London: Estates Gazette Ltd

Primarily a business tenancies journal, it includes a good range of court decisions arising under the planning legislation and some ministerial decisions. Judicial decisions are also published separately as Estates Gazette Law Reports (EGLR), a facility which commenced in 1986 and as Planning Law Reports (PLR) which commenced in 1988.

11 Useful Addresses and Telephone Numbers

In the case of local planning authorities, practitioners should consult the Longman *Directory of Local Authorities* or Shaw's *Directory of Local Authorities* to obtain details of the London borough councils, metropolitan district councils, county councils, district councils and (in Wales) the county borough councils. All of these authorities are local planning authorities.

Where contact is required with central government the following address should be used:

Department of the Environment, Transport and the Regions
Eland House
Bressenden Place
London
SW1E 5DU
Tel: 020 7890 3000

In all matters relating to planning appeals, the following address should be used:

Planning Inspectorate
Tollgate House
Houlton Street
Bristol
BS2 9DJ
Tel: 0117 7944 3945

For enforcement appeals, the following address should be used:

Department of the Environment, Transport and the Regions
(PLUP 2)
Tollgate House
Houlton Street
Bristol
BS2 9DJ
Tel: 0117 987 8754

In respect of all matters affecting land in Wales, the following address should be used:

The National Assembly for Wales
Cathays Park
Cardiff
CF1 3NQ
Tel: 01222 825111

Other useful addresses and telephone numbers are as follows:

Historic Buildings and Monuments Commission
('English Heritage')
Fortress House
23 Savile Row
London
W1X 2HE
Tel: 020 7734 6010

Commission for the New Towns
Glen House
Stag Place
Victoria
London
SW1E 5AJ
Tel: 020 7828 7722

Commission for Local Administration
Beverley House
17 Shipton Road
York
YO3 6FZ
Tel: 01904 663200

Countryside Agency
30–32 Southampton Street
London
WC2E 7RA
Tel: 020 7240 2771

Nature Conservancy Council for England
('English Nature')
Northminster House
Peterborough
PE1 1UA
Tel: 01733 455000

Environment Agency
Rio House,
Waterside Drive,
Aztec West,
Almondsbury
Bristol
BS12 4UD
Tel: 01454 624400

Countryside Council for Wales
Headquarters
Plas Penrhos
Ffordd Penrhos
Bangor
Gwynedd
LL57 2LQ
Tel: 01248 385500

Treasury Solicitor
Queen Anne's Chambers
28 Broadway
London
SW1H 9JS
Tel: 020 72103000